INSTITUTIONAL STRUCTURES OF FEELING

George Marcus, Sharon Traweek,
Richard Handler, and Vera Zolberg, *Series Editors*

Culture

and the
Ad

Exploring Otherness
in the
World of Advertising

William M. O'Barr

Westview Press
Boulder • San Francisco • Oxford

Institutional Structures of Feeling

Published in 1994 in the United States of America by Westview Press, Inc., 5500 Central Avenue, Boulder, Colorado 80301-2877, and in the United Kingdom by Westview Press, 36 Lonsdale Road, Summertown, Oxford OX2 7EW

Library of Congress Cataloging-in-Publication Data
O'Barr, William M.
   Culture and the ad : exploring otherness in the world of
advertising / William M. O'Barr.
      p.   cm. — (Institutional structures of feeling)
   Includes bibliographical references and index.
   ISBN 0-8133-2196-4 (cloth). — ISBN 0-8133-2197-2 (paper)
      1. Advertising—Social aspects—United States—History.
2. Minorities in advertising—United States—History.   3. Mass media
and race relations—United States—History.   I. Title.   II. Series.
HF5813.U602   1994
659.1'042—dc20
                                                                    93-44451
                                                                    CIP

Printed and bound in the United States of America

  ∞   The paper used in this publication meets the requirements of the American National
      Standard for Permanence of Paper for Printed Library Materials Z39.48-1984.

10   9   8   7   6   5   4   3   2

Contents

Preface

IN ORDER to make this book as accessible as possible, I depart from many conventions of academic scholarship. For one thing, I avoid technical terminology and keep brief the discussion of the pedigrees of ideas. For another, I keep references to those I believe are the most helpful and have placed them in the Bibliographic Notes that follow each chapter. There are no foot- or endnotes as such.

I hope that these aberrations will not lead to the hasty conclusion that this book is neither serious nor scholarly. On the contrary, I am striving to make things easier for less-experienced readers who are often overwhelmed by the usual conventions of scholarship. The Bibliographic Notes will guide those who want cross-references to other theoreticians in order to read further on their own. I especially recommend Judith Williamson's *Decoding Advertisements* (1978) and Robert Goldman's *Reading Ads Socially* (1992) as useful introductions to the broader scholarship on advertising in its social and cultural context. More experienced readers will realize that I am heavily influenced by both Marxism and semiotic theory, and I invite them to recast my arguments in such terms as they find useful.

I have struggled over the vantage from which to write this book, in particular how I ought best to situate myself with regard to both the subject and my readers. I have tried to allow my own experiences to inform but not overpower the analysis. I often use the first-person singular pronoun to signify this. I usually avoid the plural in order not to impose any particular reading of what I have to say. Indeed, I believe deeply in the multiplicity of meanings, a point I develop and argue with reference to the interpretation of advertisements.

The problem at hand is a bit more complicated. Sometimes I find no alternative to using *we* in the text. I use it to establish a contrast between the domestic and the foreign, between the self and others, between us and them. For this, using *we* is critical.

Additionally, I sometimes attempt to speak for all of us who stand in opposition to organized, professional advertising. In this case, I use *we* to mean we consumers, we magazine readers, and we television viewers. I specifically mean to contrast people outside the advertising establishment and those who are the copywriters, the corporate advertisers, the salespeople, the models in advertisements, and even the advertisements themselves—all of which purport in one way or another to tell us how to think, how to be, and how to live our lives. In these contexts, I seek to articulate a voice on behalf of ordinary people who stand in a particular relationship to advertising and advertisements.

Some friends and colleagues who read this book in earlier drafts pointed out that my arguments often seem directed to the white mainstream of American society rather than the diversity of people who are members of the real American public. How, they asked, did I justify this in the age of multiculturalism? I wish it were simple and easy to address this issue. I can only explain that in this study I follow the lead of advertising itself, which has tended throughout the twentieth century to treat the American public as a colorless, English-speaking mass audience of rather uniform tastes, preferences, and sensibilities. I am glad that this is changing, but as I argue in the latter chapters, this is more a matter of economic necessity than of cultural goodwill. Most fundamentally, this is a book about the process of treating people as different from the mainstream and as *other*. Thus, I direct my argument primarily toward the audience that advertising has defined as the mainstream because I believe that it is they who most need to hear and consider my argument and its significance for their lives. Those who have been defined as outside this mainstream know from experience what I am trying to say.

Finally, I caution my readers not to expect a linear argument here, one where each chapter builds straightforwardly on the previous one toward some specific goal in the conclusion. Rather, what I do here is to set the subject before the reader and offer tools and encouragement for examining it from many perspectives and vantages. In the end, these multiple viewings shape a rounded, holistic view that, I believe, is deeper than any single perspective would offer for this subject. In the early chapters, I take on the role of interpreter, making many suggestions about how to read and decode advertisements depicting foreigners. As the book progresses, I assume that an empowered reader can use these tools and conduct the finest, most relevant analysis on his or her own. That is why I choose in Chapter 5 to encourage examination of tourist photographs (either one's own or someone else's) rather than ask the reader to take my word for what such artifacts show. Then in Chapter 6 I ask the reader to join me in the process of figuring out the social meaning of ads. After all, this self-centered interpretation is how most advertisements are understood everyday. In Chapter 7 I try to turn the tables on the reader to evoke a situation that creates an empathetic appreciation of how the usual subjects of advertisements respond to its representations of their lives and their cultures.

The model for understanding advertisements developed here can be easily transferred and applied elsewhere. I encourage readers to take up the issues in advertising that concern them most. As a cultural anthropologist, I report in the following pages on my efforts to do just that.

William M. O'Barr

Acknowledgments

OF THE MANY STUDENTS and colleagues who have read versions of this book and offered critical insights along the way, I thank especially Kathryn Barrett-Gaines, Donald Brenneis, Laura Brousseau, Richard Chalfen, Claire O'Barr Culver, Brian Denton, Donna Longo DiMichele, Virginia Dominguez, David Fisher, Melinda Frank, Ernestine Friedl, Ellen Gartrell, Bill Gentner, Jennifer Grace, Miriam Hirsch, Miguel Korzenewicz, Wendy Luttrell, Jean O'Barr, John Riedy, Amy Thomas, and John Wilson. Jennifer Hirsch provided invaluable assistance with the translations of the Japanese-language advertisements. I also wish to thank—even though I cannot possibly name them all—the hundreds of Duke students whose questions, comments, and essays in my courses on advertising and society have helped shape the arguments in this book. This book is dedicated to them and to those whom I hope to teach in the future. It was their interest and encouragement that sustained the research on which this book is based.

W.M.O.

1

Analyzing Social Ideology in Advertisements

WHENEVER WE ENCOUNTER old advertisements, we never assume that they speak to us as potential consumers of what they promote. Instead, we marvel at what they offered for sale, the claims and associations they made, and the life-styles they depicted. If we come across old issues of, say, the *National Geographic* from the 1920s in an attic or secondhand bookshop, we may find ourselves captivated by the advertisements as a window onto history. We take time to read the fine print for details about a 104-day cruise to South America and Africa that cost only $1,500. We may wonder just who could afford to take such a cruise and imagine for a moment life aboard a great ocean liner or think about visiting exotic destinations. After a little while we turn the page and draw the magazine close in order to examine the details of the intricately carved Grebe Synchrophase radio cabinet with its "unrivaled" tone, and we wonder whether we ever saw one. Further along we linger over the 1929 Packard, outfitted with its running boards and "unique" shock-absorbing system. For such advertisements, we are an accidental, unexpected, and unanticipated audience. We know that they were created for their contemporaneous audience, not for those of us who might stumble onto them at some point in the future. We readily treat such old advertisements as cultural documents and establish ourselves as a critical audience for them.

By contrast, our relationship with contemporary advertisements is more primary. We know that we are members of their intended audience and that we must decide in each encounter whether an advertisement is relevant and whether we wish to fol-

low its recommendations. Many of us deny that we are much affected by the advertisements that appear in the magazines we read and the television programs we watch. Some of us even go so far as to maintain that we despise advertising, pay little attention to it, and actively avoid advertisements whenever possible. We claim to hurry through the advertising sections of magazines and newspapers, and we tout our skills at zapping television commercials. The more suspicious among us maintain constant guard against covert advertising tactics designed to overpower our resistance. Acts of saying no to contemporary advertisements, of denying their relevance, and of refusing their advice differ distinctly from the attention we more willingly pay to old ones.

In this book I explore advertisements from the past and from abroad in order to develop a more critical posture toward those we must deal with every day. By stepping momentarily beyond the boundaries of the present and the local, we learn to ask questions about contemporary advertisements that parallel those we more easily ask about older ones. In this analysis I focus on those defined as outsiders (foreigners in particular, but also Americans who are sometimes treated like foreigners: African Americans and Native Americans). My primary historical context is twentieth-century American advertising, although I give some consideration to representations of Westerners in contemporary Japanese advertisements. But the analytic framework I propose and the kinds of questions I ask are not restricted to this specific topic or time period. They are general ones that illuminate and make plain ideological premises about society and culture that are embedded throughout the discourse of advertising.

The main argument developed in this book is that the representations of foreigners and other categories of outsiders who appear in advertisements provide paradigms for relations between members of advertising's intended audience and those defined as outside it. These paradigms constitute an ideological guide for relations between the self and others, between us and them. The most frequently depicted qualities of such relationships are hierarchy, dominance, and subordination.

In the chapters that follow, I consider the models that advertisements provide to instruct us about others and our relations with them. I examine such depictions in some different time periods to determine whether apparent changes reflect fundamental alterations in the social ideology of advertising. Additionally, I search for evidence of compliance with the instructions that are given in advertisements. This is no simple matter, but I am not content only to imagine what the members of an audience may think or to speculate about whether a reader's actions correspond in any way to models provided in advertisements. Even if I cannot expect to find all the answers, I am committed to looking for ways to move beyond merely suspecting how audiences respond, a shortcoming common to most critical studies of advertisements.

In this chapter I lay the groundwork for these considerations by dealing with five issues. First, I define two key terms and concepts used in this book: ideology and discourse. Second, I propose three analytic questions that facilitate the examination of social ideologies in the discourse of advertising. Third, I consider the problem of interpreting advertisements, which is critical to deciphering the meanings of their representational forms. Fourth, I explore the nature of intended and unintended audiences for advertisements and consider the circumstances under which such boundaries may shift. Finally, I examine conceptions of foreigners in the world of advertising in order to understand how advertising creates its own internal categories of otherness.

Ideology and Discourse

During the 1980s the terms *ideology* and *discourse* gained wide currency in the social sciences and humanities. Their broad adoption signified both a shift in issues of concern to academic researchers and some new ways of talking about old interests. And like any terms in wide usage, they can and often do mean somewhat different things in different contexts. In this book I use them in quite specific ways.

By *ideology* I mean ideas that buttress and support a particular distribution of power in society. Ideology is political by its very nature. In the former Soviet Union, for example, state-sponsored propaganda attempted to instruct the public about issues of patriotism, community, and the social order. That ideology—the ideas expressed in support of the state—repressed other ideologies that sought to change who was in control as well as to portray alternative visions about society. Removed as we are in time and place, we easily comprehend the ideological nature of Soviet propaganda.

It is often more difficult to see those ideas that operate in a similar manner closer to home, those that buttress and support the social and political system within which we live. The critical theorist Raymond Williams (1980) calls advertising "the official art of capitalist society." In doing so, he points out how advertising operates ideologically in the West. It is art that is both sponsored by and supportive of capitalism. In encouraging all manner of consumption, advertising helps support an economy of mass production. It encourages, cajoles, and even demands that we buy and consume. Were we to minimize consumption, the fundamental nature of our social order would be challenged. Thus, advertising conveys ideas that are political and system maintaining. Such ideas are ideological in nature.

In this book I examine in particular social ideologies, that is, ideas of an ideological sort that are about society: who is in charge, how society is or ought to be, who is powerful, who is weak, who is dominant, who is subordinate, and so forth. When I use *ideology,* I generally mean ideas contained in advertising that support and buttress the social order of a society based on mass production and consumption.

By *discourse* I mean a flow of ideas that are connected to one another. *Discourse* can refer to related ideas that an author develops in a written text or that occur in a conversation between two people. In the case of advertising, I mean something broader. When referring to the discourse of advertising, I mean the flow of representations about commodities and society over a period of time, even as long as a century or more.

This discourse of advertising is roughly connected in that any advertisement is actively a part of a larger flow of such messages. Sometimes one advertisement makes specific reference to another or to ideas that have been discussed in previous advertisements. New advertisements do not exist in a vacuum. They acknowledge and refer to what has gone before them. They are a part of a larger flow, a discourse of advertising.

Following Michel Foucault, theorists usually reserve the term *discourse* for ideas that involve society in some way. Foucault himself was interested in questions such as how ideas about illness or marriage at any point in time are related to a body of other ideas that have preceded them. Our conventions and social practices have histories, he argued. He marked as discourse those flows of ideas over time that depict society and its order.

When we speak of the discourse of advertising, it is helpful to make a further distinction between two types of discourse—only one of which is social in nature. In this book I use *primary discourse* to refer to ideas in advertising about goods and services. These are the messages that advertising openly purports to convey: This detergent gets clothes cleaner, this cereal tastes better, this car goes faster. I use the term *secondary discourse* to refer to ideas about society and culture contained in advertisements. These ideas emerge in the context of showing how the detergent works, how the cereal is eaten, and how the car functions. In depicting the context of use of a commodity, the advertisements also depict a number of things about society, such

as who does the laundry, who prepares breakfast while someone else sits at the table, and who drives and who rides as passengers in a car. These secondary messages form an important discourse about society. From a marketing point of view, these are incidental messages that serve only to show how a product works. Nonetheless, in doing their primary work, advertisements also repeat such secondary themes and unwittingly construct a discourse about society along the way.

Three Analytic Issues

In studying the social and cultural ideologies in advertising, I have found it instructive to pose three related analytic questions. The answers to them show how advertising constructs idealized images of people, depicts their patterns of interacting with others, and positions them in the social hierarchy. Asking and answering these questions is the fundamental research method for the chapters that follow.

Idealized Images

The first question asks, What is the idealized image of people in a particular social category? This question can be asked of a single advertisement, but it is more instructively applied to a large number of depictions. "The American woman," "Arabs," or any social category can be examined this way. By looking for the recurrent themes in how advertising portrays such people, we begin to understand the idealized images constructed in the world of advertising. It is probable that the depictions will contain some points of difference from advertisement to advertisement. Such variations may reflect the complexity of the category itself. Other times the inconsistencies may come about because of the advertising world's limited or contradictory knowledge about such people. What is important to note is how advertising deals with issues of similarity and difference in its representations. Regularities, generalizations, and even patterns of variation in the images advertising constructs emerge from this exercise. Such an investigation constitutes the first analytic step.

Social Relationships

The second question asks, How do people in the category relate to others? In addition to assigning attributes to people, advertisements also depict social relationships. For example, if we look beyond the images of solitary American women in advertisements, we find that women are also depicted in interaction with other categories of persons: men, other women, children, salespeople, co-workers, and so on. What emerges from this second question is an understanding of the ideas about appropriate and idealized social relations in which people in the constructed category operate. Advertising first defines the category, but it quickly moves to place it in a social context. As with the first question, this second one is most productively applied to a number of advertisements rather than just a single one. From the second analytic step comes an understanding of the ideologies of social relationships that advertising constructs.

Inequality and Power

The third question follows upon the second: What is the quality of the relationships depicted? In looking for answers, we discover an important fact about social relationships depicted in the discourse of advertising: They are seldom egalitarian. Equality is not precluded as a possible message in the discourse of advertising. Rather, it is simply the case that most messages are about dominance and subordination, about power and submission to it. Advertisements depicting the social relationships of women with men readily demonstrate this: Men drive cars, women ride as passengers; men invite women out for an evening of dining and dancing, women accept and dress to conform to men's expectations; men sit at tables, women prepare food and serve it to them and to children. The contradictory representations that strike us as unusual—of men preparing food for women, of women proposing social engagements to men, of women making sexual advances to men—merely confirm the general and usual messages. Some defenders of advertising argue that representations of male-female relationships are changing to become more egalitarian, a defense that only demonstrates that such depictions in the past have usually been about inequality.

This line of questioning posits a relation between advertising and society. However, in no way does it assume a simple or straightforward relation, for example that advertising simply reflects society or that advertising molds society in its image. The truth is that advertising and society are related in both ways. Depictions of society in advertisements have their bases in the social order, and the social order is continually re-created by reference to ideals in advertisements and elsewhere about what it should be.

This three-step analytic paradigm is helpful in a variety of circumstances. It can be used to examine the construction of any category of people, their social relationships, and issues of power associated with them. With slight modification, it can even be used beyond the study of social ideologies in advertising to examine other ideologies, such as the construction of the concept of nature, the relations of people to nature, and the issues of human mastery over nature. With a little thought, we can extend questions about images, relationships, and power to a wide variety of messages in advertisements beyond the overt ones about goods and services that advertising purports to be about.

The Meaning of Advertisements

In order to understand how advertising both reflects and constitutes social order, I must come to terms with what advertisements mean to their audience. One way I might decide what advertisements mean is to interpret them as I expect their audience might. This approach is fraught with difficulty, especially if I use it exclusively, because the entire analysis hinges on my own theoretical perspectives and interpretive skills. A second possibility would be to seek out the copywriters who put the advertisements together. This approach would take up the timeworn quest for an author's own intended meaning, although it is hardly practical when dealing with large numbers of advertisements and hence different copywriters. A third possibility would be to focus attention on those who regularly do the work of interpreting advertisements—the audience itself. This approach emphasizes the collaborative nature of constructing meaning in advertising messages rather than assuming that fixed meanings are somehow inherent in advertisements. Each of these approaches has some positive aspects to commend it as well as some inherent drawbacks and limitations. Before settling on one or another of them, I examine briefly how two other scholars have dealt with the matter of interpretation.

A widely read and generally appreciated analysis of meaning in advertisements is Judith Williamson's *Decoding Advertisements* (1978). In this richly illustrated book, Williamson walks the reader through a gallery of advertisements and discusses their ideological content. Her own critical perspective is informed by a variety of theorists, including Ferdinand de Saussure, Karl Marx, Louis Althusser, Raymond Williams, Sigmund Freud, and Jacques Lacan. Williamson's pedagogic objective is to teach the naive reader how to interpret advertisements along the lines of these theorists, and many readers do find that their critical abilities are greatly developed by applying Williamson's theories: Advertisements lose whatever simple qualities they may have had and become instead texts about production and consumption in the consumer society, about the place of commodities in social life, and about the creation of needs to service an economic system that must sell what has been produced.

In addition to teaching the interpretation of advertisements, Williamson explains how advertising constructs the ideological principles that are embedded in it. For example, many advertisements borrow ideas from external sources ("referent systems") such as cultural history or concepts of nature. In the process of appropriating, reworking, and using them, advertising transforms the borrowed ideas. The advertisements for Virginia Slims cigarettes, which frequently refer to the history of women's struggle for social and economic equality in America, illustrate this process. Selected events from this struggle are retold and edited in selected ways, and progress is depicted as contemporary women's having gained the right to smoke. Similarly, hundreds of products that proclaim their "natural" qualities are in reality highly altered through complex manufacturing processes. Instances like these, Williamson claims, illustrate the construction of ideology through advertisements. The resulting distortions over the long run alter our understandings of the original ideas that were borrowed and (mis)used within advertising.

Williamson's approach to the interpretation of advertisements is founded on her goal of transforming the reader's skills. She does not treat as problematic that uninstructed readers make whatever sense they do of the thousands of advertisements populating their daily lives. Neither does she take any great interest in how the copywriters who produced the advertisements thought about their work. Instead, she assumes that a naive reader's failure to see the issues she uncovers is a false consciousness of their meaning, a falseness on which advertising depends to do its work. The approach hinges fundamentally on Williamson's own skill in applying the various theoretical perspectives to the advertisements. From the outset she bedazzles the reader by observing details and patterns in advertisements that ordinarily slip by an audience. She repeatedly points out the contradictions between what advertisements seem to say and what they really mean according to the various perspectives.

Although Williamson considers advertising's audience naive, she does not assume that its members are merely receivers of packaged messages that emanate from advertisers. Rather, she argues, the audience is implicated in the production of meaning, a collaboration that advertising continually invites:

[A] crucial feature of these odds and ends of thought used by ads is that they do not exist "independently" but in *our* thought: it is *we*, as subjects, who are appealed to as *providers* of these elements. ... For it is individual people, real people, who are the connecting link here: they, we, clearly exist in time and space, in a changing world, but also provide the arena—unconscious—for the ideological structure of ideas. This only exists inside our heads. (1978:101–102)

Despite this status of audience-as-author, Williamson's analysis is in no apparent way dependent on any evidence about what members of the audience actually think the advertisements mean. Here analysis depends entirely on her own theoretical assumptions and interpretations. She tells, but never asks, her readers what the advertisements mean. Thus, if we look behind the specific ideologies of society revealed through her approach, we find a theory about where meaning rests and how it works in advertising. Put simply, it says something like this: Naive readers who do not understand the social ideologies in advertising labor under false consciousness about their meaning. These deceptive meanings create desires for consumer goods and thus promote selling. Social theorists are privileged with the ability to decode real meaning. Naive readers may learn the decoding process and thereby develop their own abilities to derive the true meaning of advertisements.

Roland Marchand's *Advertising the American Dream* (1985) was hailed by reviewers as the most comprehensive and well-researched social history of advertising yet published. In it, Marchand examines advertising in the 1920s and 1930s, a time when the mass media helped teach new waves of immigrants how to be American. How else, he asks, did such diverse immigrant groups as East Europeans, Asians, and others come to have living rooms, bathrooms, and kitchens as well as families and aspirations that bear remarkable similarities to one another? He argues that the information provided by advertisements, and especially the rich visual imagery of advertising of this time period, played a key role.

For his analysis, Marchand develops the concept of the "social tableaus," or visual images of society appearing in advertisements, that give such information to the public. His concept of the social tableau is drawn from the *tableau vivant* (or living tableau) of the nineteenth-century theater. Marchand

reminds us that before visual images were as common as they are today, the legitimate theater functioned to give many people images of things that were known to them primarily through verbal description. It was common in the theaters of that time to enact well-known moments in history (such as Washington crossing the Delaware or the signing of the Declaration of Independence) or moods (such as summertime or young love) in living tableaus between the acts of longer theatrical programs. The curtain would rise on these enactments in which poses and scenes would remain frozen for several minutes. During these intervals, audiences could study the images—many of which they saw enacted for the first time. In the 1920s and 1930s, Marchand tells us, print advertising worked this way. A public not yet accustomed to an overkill of visual imagery paid attention to the scenes and styles enacted in advertisements. This information supplied them with the guidelines of cultural standardization that were to take place in the following decades.

Despite the attractiveness of the inferences Marchand draws about the role of advertising in twentieth-century America, there is no real evidence in this otherwise carefully documented book about what members of the audience for these advertisements actually thought about them. Additionally, there are only inferences about the relation between advertisements and behavior. When all is said and done, Marchand's approach to the meaning of advertisements shares with Williamson's its dependence on the skill of the critical interpreter. What each seeks to illuminate in the advertisements differs, but the overall approach in both instances is one of teaching critical abilities.

Marchand's analysis of advertisements is driven by his interest as a historian. He explains how he first approached advertisements as cultural documents that would help him tell a story about America in the 1920s and 1930s. As he worked with them, he came to understand that rather than being reflections of social life and cultural values in previous decades, advertisements were at best refractions. He turned instead to an investigation of advertisers (both companies producing goods for sale and advertising agencies helping promote them) and their role in the construction of the idealized world of advertisements.

For his data, Marchand reviewed thousands of advertisements appearing in magazines and newspapers as well as various documents contained in the archives of advertising agencies and corporations. From these materials he is able to piece together an impressive account of major themes in the advertisements of the period as well as an overview of the motives and objectives of the advertisers. It is unfortunate that the sources themselves do not contain much information about the intentions behind particular advertisements. Such details, interesting as they would be, seem to have been lost.

Marchand treats audience response as outside the bounds of his inquiry. Here is what he has to say about this issue:

> Advertisements present problems that differ more in degree than in kind from those involved in interpreting social reality from more conventional historical sources. We may not be able to prove the specific effects of an advertisement on its readers, but neither can we prove the effects of religious tracts, social manifestos, commemorative addresses, and political campaign speeches on their audiences. ... Advertisements merely share the characteristics of many other suspect forms of evidence about popular attitudes: ... we do not know if audiences shared or adopted the ideas presented. (1985:xviii)

Like Williamson's *Decoding Advertisements,* Marchand's book contains a theory about author, interpreter, and audience. In Marchand's case it might be summarized like this: Advertisements themselves contain a highly selected and edited view of society, one that is nonetheless helpful in comprehending social reality in the past. By examining many advertisements, one may understand these images of society. (*One* refers first and foremost to the social historian, Marchand himself, but these skills are also available to others who ask similar questions.) The substantive content of advertisements is best understood if the objectives and motives of advertisers are taken into consideration. These intentions of the authors of advertisements are generally available through the documentary record, although links between specific advertisements and authors' intentions are not possible. The interpretations of advertisements members of the audience make, as well as actions they take in response to advertisements, are inaccessible.

In this book I intend to build upon the precedents established by Williamson and Marchand. Were it not for the foundations their scholarship provides, I would have much more ground to cover. However, I seek to deal more specifically with the matter of audience response and to move beyond the limits imposed by imagining or suspecting what audiences may think. The interpretive triangle—of author, audience, and critical interpreter—is the base on which meaning is generated. Understanding how advertisements mean what they do requires attention to all three.

Meaning resides only in those who do the work of interpreting, whether they be the makers of advertisements, critical interpreters, or naive readers. To each of these, the reality is that advertisements mean what they think they mean, no more and no less. This working assumption results in an appreciation that meaning is neither uniform nor shared by all interpreters. Rather, the meaning of an advertisement can vary somewhat from interpreter to interpreter. For example, the original author who thinks up an idea for an advertisement and sees it through production has a particular understanding of what the advertisement means. That is why people who produce advertisements usually find critical assessments of their creative efforts so alien.

And what about the naive audience for an advertisement who have not read Williamson, Marchand, or a host of other treatises, including some parts of this book, which purport to explain what advertisements really mean? Are their understandings of no interest or value in comprehending how meaning works in advertising? Are they to be dismissed as only laboring under mistaken understandings and not worth bothering with?

I treat the issue of the audience's response to advertisements as problematic and attempt to include it among my considerations. There are several reasons for this. First, both the meaning of advertisements and the responses of audiences have typically been treated as monolithic. I believe that the critical understanding of meaning in advertising will be greatly enhanced by working from the opposite understanding: that different people find different meaning in advertisements (which, incidentally, has been carefully documented by generations of market researchers). Second, the production of the meaning of any text is a collaborative venture on the parts of the audience and the original author. A consideration of the role of the reader has transformed literary theory in recent years. I believe that greater attention to it can have a similar effect in studies of what advertisements mean. Third, what texts mean to their audiences can and ought to be researched rather than imagined. This investigatory attitude characterizes empirical research of all sorts, and there is every reason to consider what might be learned about advertisements and their audiences through empirical research.

In order to set the stage more fully for an approach to meaning in advertising that attempts to incorporate these considerations, I need to say a little more about the collaborative work of the audience with the other two members of the interpretive triangle: the original author and the critical interpreter.

First, there is the matter of the intentionality of the author and the collaboration of the audience with it. Whenever we ask, "What does this advertisement mean?" we imply that the advertisement has a definite and fixed meaning that is significantly related to what its creators intended it to mean. Thus, in asking what it means, we are often asking whether we have received the intended meaning of those who constructed the advertisement.

But the meaning of an advertisement is not this simple. We "read into" an advertisement additional meanings beyond those that were intended, or we may "miss the point" and think it means something else altogether. Although our talk about advertisements suggests that a discrepancy between our in-

terpretation of an advertisement and the advertiser's meaning is a failure on our part, the meaning of advertisements is actually a joint collaborative effort on the parts of the maker and the consumer. And even more fundamentally, advertisements work—in the sense of convincing us to adopt attitudes and act on them—only when the meaning is our own, whether we supplied a portion or all of it.

The question of what the advertiser meant in constructing an advertisement is a worthy one, but too much attention on it deflects our understanding of how advertisements mean what they do to us. In our interpretation of them, we may receive the meaning exactly as the author may have intended, we may adjust it in some way, or perhaps we supply a meaning at odds with the intention of those who made the advertisement. Whichever happens, the advertisement means to us exactly what we think it means—no more, no less.

Once we grasp that the consumer is the ultimate author of the meaning of an advertisement, the intentions of the makers become of secondary importance. Ultimately, they may even be irrelevant. Indeed, some contemporary advertising leaves interpretation wide open, the advertisers inviting the audience to participate, aware that what they intended may not help at all in the consumers' comprehension of the meaning. It may simply be that the intention of the maker was to create an advertisement that we would use as a skeleton to which we would add flesh and into which we would breathe life.

Examples of advertisements that work like this abound in the late twentieth century. In the late 1980s Benson and Hedges attracted considerable public attention because the meaning of its advertisements was not immediately apparent (Figure 1.1). In the first of what has become a series of untitled tableaus depicting social settings, a young man stands in pajama bottoms at some distance from a table of fully dressed men and women. They are saying something to him. One man at the table even has his glass raised. But who is the pajama man, and what connection does he have to the other people? What do any of them have to do with the cigarettes, except that they are all possibly

For people
who like
to smoke...

BENSON & HEDGES
100S

De Luxe
Ultra Lights

BENSON & HEDGES
100S

De Luxe
Ultra Lights

DELUXE
ULTRA LIGHTS
Regular
and
Menthol.

BENSON & HEDGES
because quality matters.

© Philip Morris Inc. 1988

6 mg "tar," 0.6 mg nicotine av. per cigarette, by FTC method

Figure 1.1

smokers and that this situation somehow evokes the product in its context of use with representative consumers?

This advertisement was widely discussed in the media because of the attention it generated. The connection among product, consumer, and use was too indirect to fit conventional formulas. The public asked what the advertisement meant. When the makers of the advertisement spoke up and revealed their intentions, they demonstrated how advertising works. What had apparently happened was that the actor wearing pajamas wandered off an adjacent set onto the one where the people were seated at the table. The photographer quickly took a picture of the surprised reactions of the actors. Instead of the planned photograph of social interaction, the serendipitous photo was used. And it worked as an advertising technique that got the public's attention and became the base for many additional Benson and Hedges advertisements depicting murky social gatherings for which we, as audience, must supply the meaning.

Even further away from a clear articulation of product, consumer, and use is the advertisement for Merit cigarettes appearing in Figure 1.2. This advertisement shows neither the cigarette nor its user. It makes no claim about the cigarette other than that it is flavorful, but it does not even attempt to describe what that means. The advertisement invites the audience to imagine what flavor means and to link that concept to Merit. This advertisement makes overt what is to some degree always true of every advertisement, namely, that the process of interpretation is a collaborative effort of audience and creator.

Both the Benson and Hedges and Merit advertisements illustrate how too great a concern with author intentionality can misdirect attention away from the important role that the audience plays in constructing meaning. These advertisements contain no hidden meanings. Whatever meanings they do have are supplied entirely by their audiences, not by those who construct the advertisements.

When we understand that advertising works this way, we can then ask what the makers of advertising intend. When we discover their intentions, we

are not bound by them. Indeed, we may be amused at just how far away from our interpretations they are. And because we are the authors of what the advertisements mean, we may even decide that it is they who misunderstand.

However, it is not only with the original author of the advertisement that the audience collaborates in producing meaning. The critical discourse about advertising—whether in its everyday form focusing on issues like deception, condescension, or promotion of unwanted things or in its scholarly mode exemplified by Williamson and Marchand—may also be incorporated into the audience's process of interpreting advertisements. Critical interpreters of advertising—from parents and schoolteachers to college professors and social critics—emerge in an individual's life almost as early as advertisements themselves. The audience works in conjunction with whichever such interpreters they believe and trust to collaborate once again in the production of meaning. Like those who constructed the advertisements, the critics influence but do not ultimately determine meaning.

Finally, it needs to be noted that no individual interprets an advertisement outside a broader context that supplies considerable assistance. There are rules about the license that obtains in the make-believe world of advertisements. Consumers have conversations with kitchen appliances and bathroom fixtures, underwear sprouts legs and dances, tubs of margarine talk back to them, and so forth. The symbols and representations in advertisements are related to culture more broadly, and in our interpretations we draw on our experiences elsewhere.

Foreigners and Other Outsiders in the World of Advertising

The chapters that follow focus on the representations of foreigners and certain additional categories of people who are treated as "other" by advertising. This subject has received little consideration in the critical investigation of advertising, and this would be reason enough to concentrate on it here. But in

The world's first do-it-yourself print ad.

Close your eyes and imagine the most flavorful picture you can.
Now, think "Merit." Congratulations! You've created the perfect Merit ad.
Because flavor is what Merit is all about. Merit Enriched Flavor™ delivers
real smoking satisfaction with even less tar than leading lights.
So thanks for your help. You created the perfect image for Merit.
And you saved us a bundle on expensive photography.

Enriched Flavor™ low tar. A solution with Merit.

© Philip Morris Inc. 1988

Kings: 8 mg "tar," 0.6 mg nicotine av. per cigarette by FTC method.

Figure 1.2

addition to whatever arguments might be advanced in its support, this topic also offers a special opportunity to deal with many theoretical issues perhaps more easily than might be possible with other themes.

First, a focus on foreigners and other outsiders facilitates an understanding of certain issues about advertisements and their audiences. Most importantly, it demonstrates that advertising defines the boundaries of its audience in line with the boundaries of the markets for the commodities it promotes. Within the bounds of its audience, advertising is deeply concerned with the appropriateness and even the morality of its representations. It takes care not to offend the members of its audience, lest offense result in lost sales. For those defined as outside the market—and thus outside the audience—these considerations do not apply.

Second, members of advertising's audience create some important records that demonstrate the degree of congruence between the representations shown within advertisements and those created outside of but as a result of advertisements. Advertisements that depict foreigners, I argue, depict ideologies about relationships between us and them. When tourists visit foreign locations, they create a set of representations about other people in the form of tourist photographs. These records, produced by members of advertising's audience, can be compared to the representations within advertisements themselves. This opportunity is to some degree unique.

At the outset of this consideration, it is helpful to keep in mind some of the different ways in which foreigners are of concern to marketers and advertisers. First, they are sometimes a market for American-made goods. Second, they can be a part of the commodity itself, as, for example, when an advertisement concerns travel to another country. Third, their images may be appropriated and used in contexts that have little or nothing to do with the origin, manufacture, or use of the advertised item. When foreigners are thought of as a market, advertising emphasizes the similarity of their lives and desires to Americans. When foreigners are treated as a commodity, it is their differences and the exoti-

cism of their lives that are emphasized. When their images are appropriated into the service of selling commodities hardly related to them in reality, advertising is little concerned with the accuracy of the images it constructs.

Full-scale concern by advertising agencies with foreign markets emerged in the late 1920s in conjunction with the expansion of American manufacturing operations overseas. Prior to that time, advertising of American-made goods in foreign markets was managed either by a foreign-language (usually only Spanish) department of the big New York and Philadelphia agencies or by an agency specializing in export advertising. In either case the copy was prepared in the United States, translated by bilingual employees, and sent abroad for publication in newspapers and magazines.

In the years following the end of World War I, General Motors expanded its overseas manufacturing operations. This expansion initiated fundamental changes in the way American advertising agencies would deal with foreign markets. In 1927 GM's American advertising agency, J. Walter Thompson, began setting up branch offices near the manufacturing plants with the objective of assisting their client in making the American car the world standard. Within five years, JWT opened offices in more than twenty countries in Europe, Latin America, Africa, and Asia. On the heels of GM and JWT, N. W. Ayer and Son opened foreign offices in the countries where Ford had its major manufacturing and marketing operations. In short order, Standard Oil and its advertising agency, McCann-Erickson, did the same thing.

What the advertising agencies had to come to terms with as a result of this expansion overseas was the significance of language and cultural differences. Could the same basic advertising principles be applied everywhere, or were differences between people such that different principles would be needed? Documents from the period reflect the efforts of the advertising agencies to come up with answers. As the agencies pushed to make advertisements more sensitive to local differences, their client companies pushed for more uniform advertising, attempting to minimize expenses.

Through these negotiations emerged a strong conviction that differences between languages and cultures are more superficial than fundamental. Both sides agreed that people everywhere had the same basic needs and objectives. Transportation was needed in Argentina as well as the United States, yeast and baking powder worked in South Africa in the same way they did in England, and beauty was as much a concern to women in New Zealand as it was to women in Belgium. Advertisers found minor variations in how these issues are best addressed locally, but they concluded that underlying motives to which advertising speaks are much the same everywhere. Thus, the agencies concluded that they were in the business of assisting their clients in identifying and satisfying the unifying desires of people in markets all over the world. This belief about the fundamental similarity of people everywhere persists in contemporary advertising and marketing.

By contrast, advertising conceives of foreigners in terms of their differences from us when it treats them in the context of travel to other countries. The circuslike curiosity of others (rather than the discovery that superficial difference masks more fundamental commonality) is a recurrent theme in twentieth-century travel advertisements. Advertising justifies its interest in differences by claiming that this is what travelers seek. Whichever comes first, the culture or the ad, a cycle is quickly established: Advertisements depict differences because consumers expect them, and consumers expect differences because travel advertisements play them up. When advertising conceives of foreigners as commodities rather than as markets, it makes very different assumptions about them.

The appropriation of the images of foreigners for use in contexts that have no real connection to the origin, manufacture, or use of the advertised item is based on a consideration of the foreigners as neither market nor commodity. Rather, foreigners—or some aspects of their cultures—provide convenient imagery for advertising to use in its primary business of selling goods and services. Such gratuitous uses of these referents soon constitute primary knowledge about others. Images of dozing Mexicans and of penny-pinching Scots have been used countless times to communicate themes of relaxation and thrift, but they have also helped communicate ideas about the people of Mexico and Scotland.

In this book I analyze representations of foreigners in both commodified and appropriated contexts. I argue that it is important to keep in mind advertisers' ideas about foreigners as markets, because they provide important insight into understanding the circumstances under which the representations change. When foreigners cease to be merely a part of foreign tourism and become business partners and consumers, this expansion occasions increased sensitivity to the qualities in such representations.

Although I start this investigation by considering the more clear-cut case of non-Americans as foreigners, I find it impossible to maintain a distinction between foreigners and all sorts of "others" (such as Native Americans and immigrant ethnic groups) who have shared similar fates. Domestic travel to government reservations for Native Americans, less commonly a subject for advertising than foreign travel, has many parallels to foreign travel. And the iconography of Eskimo and African-American cultures along with many others has been used to sell ice cream, pancakes, and countless other commodities.

Outline of the Book

The central issue I investigate is the ideologies about "others" that are constructed within the discourse of advertising. These representations constitute a significant sector of popular representations of others. Additional representations are found in books, movies, television, and other popular cultural forms. I share with Williamson, Marchand, and other critical scholars the goal of conveying to my readers what I believe advertisements tell us about social ideologies. I believe that this goal is best accomplished by dealing with many aspects of this subject and in somewhat different ways. The chapters that follow do not tell a linear narrative guided by progress through time. Rather, I have elected to set the general issue before the reader and to examine it from a number of perspectives in the hope that these different vantages will produce a rounded understanding.

In Chapter 2 I look at some of the instructions that advertisements give for representing others. These instructions are clearly depicted in advertisements for travel photography, which tend to display explicitly the relationship between the visitor and the visited and to provide models (in the form of sample photographs) of what tourists' photographs should look like. In these photographs are displayed the issues of images, relationships, and power that constitute social ideologies about otherness.

In Chapter 3 I examine the advertisements that appeared in the twelve issues of the *National Geographic* published in 1929. Any particular year, set of issues, or publication might be analyzed to determine how foreigners are represented in its advertisements. In seeking a text to illustrate the issues associated with foreigners in advertising, I first chose the *National Geographic* magazine because it is widely read and tends to be saved longer than most other magazines. And for many people who are not privy to the more restricted discourse of academic anthropology, this magazine—both its articles and the parallel texts in its advertisements—has been their window onto the exotic and the foreign. When I first began working on the research project that has culminated in this book, I intended to limit myself to advertisements published in the *National Geographic.* However, some issues I treat could not have been included under that plan. I say all this to emphasize how *any* magazine, *any* year would do. Representations of foreigners and outsiders of all sorts are by no means restricted to the *National Geographic.* I chose 1929 because it was convenient to do so. Travel abroad was widely advertised as were cameras for personal use. The depression had not yet set in, World War I was over, and World War II was far in the future. I invite readers to substitute other publications and time periods and to ask the questions I ask in Chapter 3. The volume and specific content of advertisements

may differ, but I suspect that the basic observations about how foreigners are represented in the discourse of advertising will not.

In Chapter 4 I do what I have just proposed by looking at the representations of foreigners in contemporary print advertisements from the late 1980s and early 1990s. The main conclusion I draw is that the basic patterns of representing foreigners are not fundamentally different from what I found in the 1929 *National Geographic* advertisements. In fact, I believe that the general patterns have not changed much over the entire twentieth century. This claim about consistency rather than change is strengthened by comparing the representations of foreigners to representations of African Americans and of gender roles over this same period. A thorough study of this topic would be a wonderful but monumental undertaking. I deal with it in a small way by trying to show in Chapter 6 how representations of African Americans have in fact changed during the twentieth century, primarily as a result of the civil rights movement, which in turn moved African Americans from the status of marginal economic concern to marketers and advertisers to a minority within American society whose spending patterns as well as sensitivities about representations of their lives emerged as real concerns.

In Chapter 5 I begin my attempt to move myself out of the central role as critical interpreter. The topic for this chapter is audience responses to the models and paradigms of representation that I believe advertisements depicting foreigners hold up before us. In this chapter I ask the reader to collaborate in the analysis of audience response by examining a set of someone's travel photographs. They can be the reader's own photographs or those of anyone else; even better would be an examination of more than one set. The question I pose is simple and straightforward: To what degree do people take photographs that replicate the images and relationships depicted in advertisements? I have asked this question of my own photographs and of those of other families, and I have twice taught a seminar in which participants undertook such analyses on their own. These firsthand experiences were powerful teachers, and I have decided to invite readers to discover the degree of congruence directly and to ask what it means. In Chapter 5 I propose the guidelines for such an investigation. There is another reason as well why I prefer this approach to merely reporting on the travelers whose photographs I have studied. It is that this kind of inquiry also demonstrates amply that members of advertising's audience vary in important ways in their responses and their mimicking of patterns. These differences appear to be both individually and socially patterned.

In Chapter 6 I try to involve readers more fully in making decisions about the representations of others in advertisements. I could continue to say what I think is represented in the advertisements, but it makes little difference unless the reader comes to these conclusions as well. Changes in the representations of African Americans in advertisements over the twentieth century are the overt subject of this chapter. An equally important matter is my sharing with and even handing over primarily to the reader the decision about what social ideologies are conveyed through the advertisements. If I have been successful in earlier chapters, then some of what I have had to say may be useful to the reader in arriving at these decisions.

In Chapter 7 I further explore the matter of audience response by looking at the depictions of the Japanese in American advertisements and of Westerners in Japanese advertisements. My goal here is to show how representations about the Japanese, in contrast to representations of "others" more generally, have changed over the twentieth century in the world of American advertising as Japan has gone from utterly exotic to tourist destination and the Japanese from enemies to business partners and even owners of parts of America. A second goal is to demonstrate to an American audience what the process of "othering" is all about by looking at a situation in which white Westerners are the object of that process. As in the two previous chapters, I hope to involve the reader in the critical assessment of social ideology in advertising.

Finally, in Chapter 8, I turn to the future, in particular to ask about the circumstances under which the patterns of representing foreigners may be expected to change. In addition, I make a final effort to engage the reader in a broader response to advertisements.

Bibliographic Notes

Two important critical works of advertising are Judith Williamson, *Decoding Advertisements: Ideology and Meaning in Advertising* (London: Marion Boyars, 1978), and Roland Marchand, *Advertising the American Dream: Making Way for Modernity, 1920–1940* (Berkeley: University of California Press, 1985). Other important critical scholars of advertising include: Diane Barthel, *Putting on Appearances: Gender and Advertising* (Philadelphia: Temple University Press, 1988); John Berger, *Ways of Seeing* (Harmondsworth: Penguin, 1972); Stuart Ewen, *Captains of Consciousness: Advertising and the Social Roots of the Consumer Culture* (New York: McGraw-Hill, 1976); Richard Wightman Fox and T. J. Jackson Lears, eds., *The Culture of Consumption: Critical Essays in American History, 1880–1980* (New York: Pantheon, 1983); Erving Goffman, *Gender Advertisements* (Cambridge: Harvard University Press, 1976); William Leiss, Stephen Kline, and Sut Jhally, *Social Communication in Advertising: Persons, Products, and Images of Well-being* (New York: Methuen, 1986); Michael Schudson, *Advertising, the Uneasy Persuasion: Its Dubious Impact on American Society* (New York: Basic Books, 1984); Raymond Williams, "Advertising: The Magic System," in his *Problems in Materialism and Culture* (London: Verso, 1980); and Rosalind Williams, *Dream Worlds: Mass Consumption in Late Nineteenth-Century France* (Berkeley: University of California Press, 1982). Especially important theoretical treatments of advertising that attempt to place it in the context of contemporary social and critical theories are Robert Goldman, *Reading Ads Socially* (New York: Routledge, 1992) and Daniel Miller, *Material Culture and Mass Consumption* (Oxford: Blackwell, 1987).

Foucault's influence on the thinking of humanists and social scientists stems from his several books in which he developed ideas about social discourse. His best-known works include *The Archaeology of Knowledge*, trans. A. M. Sheridan Smith (New York: Pantheon, 1972), *The Birth of the Clinic: An Archaeology of Medical Perception*, trans. A. M. Sheridan Smith (New York: Pantheon, 1973), *Madness and Civilization: A History of Insanity in the Age of Reason*, trans. Richard Howard (New York: Pantheon, 1965), and *The History of Sexuality*, trans. Robert Hurley (New York: Pantheon, 1978).

Reader-response criticism that focuses on the role of the reader and literary audience has emerged as a competing approach to literary criticism in the latter decades of the twentieth century. The essays in Jane P. Tompkins, ed., *Reader-Response Criticism: From Formalism to Post-structuralism* (Baltimore: Johns Hopkins University Press, 1980) provide a good introduction to the approach. In her introduction to the volume, the editor explains the field:

> Reader-response criticism is not a conceptually unified critical position, but a term that has come to be associated with the work of critics who use the words *reader, the reading process,* and *response* to mark out an area for investigation. In the context of Anglo-American criticism, the reader-response movement arises in direct opposition to the New Critical dictum issues by Wimsatt and Beardsley in "The Affective Fallacy" (1949): "The Affective Fallacy is a confusion between the poem and its results. ... It begins by trying to derive the standard of criticism from the psychological effects of a poem and ends in impressionism and relativism" (p. 21). Reader-response critics would argue that a poem cannot be understood apart from its results. Its "effects," psychological and otherwise, are essential to any accurate description of its meaning, since that meaning has no effective existence outside of its realization in the mind of a reader. (1980:ix)

The issues associated with the internationalization of American advertising in the late 1920s have not, to my knowledge, been fully dealt with in print. The brief analytic comments I have made in this chapter are based on extensive research in the archives of the J. Walter Thompson Company (now housed in Perkins Library at Duke University) and additional work in the less comprehensive in-house archives of N. W. Ayer & Son in New York. McCann-Erickson does not maintain an official archive open to outside researchers, but some inferences about its activities are possible through the archival records kept by JWT and N. W. Ayer as well as the public relations department of the agency.

Instructions in Representing Others

ONE OF THE GREATEST obstacles to understanding the secondary discourse of advertising is our resistance to advertisements. We see so many every day that most of us actively turn our attention away. This inattention is a problem advertisers recognize as evidenced by frequent discussions in trade journals on the challenges of attracting consumer attention. But disavowal of advertising's influence in our lives usually means that we also leave it unexamined. In dismissing it, we deny its influence.

My primary goal in this chapter is to initiate an alteration in our relationship to the representational forms of advertising by defamiliarizing these texts and treating them as worthy of investigating. To accomplish this I use a set of advertisements from the past for which no contemporary reader is a part of the intended audience. Because they are old and out-of-date as selling messages, it is easy to treat them as cultural documents rather than as something to be contended with or purposefully dismissed.

The advertisements examined in this chapter instruct us in ways of seeing and relating to other people and their cultures. When they first appeared, these advertisements attempted to sell travel photography. They depict both the touristic experience and the photographic record frequently generated in association with it.

I selected the advertisements from two sources: the *National Geographic* magazine and an archival collection of Kodak print advertisements. I chose them because they illustrate how to use cameras and what to photograph in touristic contexts. They frequently depict both how the finished photo-

graphs should look and ways to display or show them. Many advertisements for travel photography deal with foreign peoples and cultures, offering blueprints for their readers to use in constructing their own touristic experiences and about representing otherness.

Before we examine the advertisements themselves, I would like to place both photography and foreign travel in historical context. This will assist in distinguishing conceptually between those changes across time that reflect fundamental alterations in models for interacting with others and those due primarily to the evolution of the camera and tourism.

Although photography was widely known and liked in the latter decades of the nineteenth century, it was not until the 1890s that it became generally available to nonprofessionals as a device to record the details of their personal experiences and family lives. Prior to that time, portraits of individuals and groups as well as visual records of such major events as weddings, births, and graduations were usually commemorated in studio photographs taken by professionals. The cumbersome equipment needed to take pictures restricted locational photography. Around 1890, technological advancements made smaller, portable cameras available to the public. Along with other manufacturers of photographic equipment, Kodak began marketing cameras to nonprofessional, or amateur, photographers. Their slogan for the box camera, "You press the button, we do the rest," attempted to make it clear that the camera, previously restricted in use because of the clumsy equipment involved, could now be operated by virtually anyone. Some of the first cameras Kodak offered to the public contained rolls of film sufficient for taking 100 pictures. When the film had been exposed, the entire camera was returned to the factory for processing, printing, and reloading.

Camera advertisements from this period, such as Figure 2.1, provided this information to prospective buyers. The content of this advertisement is typical of those that follow the introduction of a new product or service. When the product is unfamiliar, advertising plays the role of instructing potential consumers about how the advertised item would fit into their lives. Once the usage is widely understood, advertisements serve more commonly to remind consumers about the availability of the product and to reinforce brand identity. Camera manufacturers, however, found instructional advertising necessary beyond the introduction of amateur photographic equipment. Once people owned cameras, they needed to be told what their pictures ought to look like. This type of instruction became the predominant subject matter of camera advertisements during the first half of the twentieth century and even characterizes many recent advertisements that continue to demonstrate an even wider role for photography in American life.

By the end of World War I, most advertisements were heavily illustrated. But until the 1930s the majority of these illustrations were drawings rather than photographs. Camera advertising followed this general pattern by using drawings both to depict the ease of using amateur photographic equipment and to provide models for photographs. Only in the 1930s did camera advertisements begin to incorporate photographs as illustrations.

From the early decades of this century, advertisements have promoted both still and movie cameras as essential items for travelers. The camera has been touted as a device to simplify the keeping of a travel diary and as a mechanism to bring home, preserve, and display photographic souvenirs. Elaborate visuals, first in the form of line drawings and later as photographs, have instructed readers about what to photograph as tourists as well as how to view and display their pictures back at home.

Today the use of the camera is distributed widely across social classes in America to the point where a great many people regularly record on film such events as birthdays, holidays, and vacations. Technical changes throughout the century (e.g., less expensive and easier-to-operate cameras, self-processing cameras, faster film, and videotape) have increased the availability, quality, and flexibility of picture taking for the American public. Advertisements have continued to announce advances in technology and to depict the situations and contexts in which the camera might be used. Both messages have been communicated so successfully that the camera is now an ordinary part of American culture, and many of the models in the advertisements have been thoroughly emulated. For example, many if not most Americans consider the perfect birthday photograph to be a snapshot that freezes the action of blowing out the candles on the cake. The repeated depictions of this particular scene in Kodak advertising has helped provide the standard against which many Americans evaluate their own skills as photographers and chroniclers of life's experiences. Similarly, advertisements for touristic photographs have provided instructions for what to see when visiting other people and places and how these experiences should be recorded on film.

Like the camera, tourism has evolved considerably over a similar time period. Until the mid-nineteenth century, when the expansion of railways and the building of large ocean liners made travel more accessible to greater numbers of people, foreign travel had largely been restricted to diplomats, statesmen, missionaries, explorers, and the very wealthy. Like other consumer goods and services that were mass produced and made widely available, excursions away from home became a commodity offered for sale to the public.

Daniel Boorstin, librarian of Congress and eclectic scholar of American culture, has written at length about the democratization and commodification of tourism that began in the nineteenth century. To explain what has emerged since about 1850, he draws a conceptual distinction between *travel* and *tourism*. Before the mid-nineteenth century,

The Kodak Camera

"You press the button, -
- - - *we do the rest."*

The only camera that anybody can use without instructions. Send for the Primer free.

A Transparent Film
For Roll Holders.

The announcement is hereby made that the undersigned have perfected a process for making transparent flexible films for use in roll holders and Kodak Cameras.

The new film is as thin, light and flexible as paper and as transparent as glass. It requires *no stripping*, and it is wound on spools for roll holders.

It will be known as *Eastman's Transparent Film*. Circulars and samples will be sent to any address on receipt of 4 cents in stamps.

Price $25.00—Loaded for 100 Pictures.

The Eastman Dry Plate and Film Co.

ROCHESTER, N. Y.

Figure 2.1

travel (a term rooted in Old English, French, and Latin words that indicate that it was laborious and difficult; related to *travail*) connoted adventure, but it included the expectation that such adventure would require toilsome effort. Prior to the nineteenth century, leaving home was an uncertain venture. For example, on the continent of Europe, amenities were few, roads were virtually nonexistent, and communications were limited. In Great Britain it was customary for the sons of affluent families to complete their educations by heading off for two or three years, making the grand circuit of European capitals and encountering other cultures firsthand. To other locations and by large numbers of people, travel was virtually unknown. For those who were able to go, the experience was informative; it expanded the mind, but it was work, not play.

By contrast, tourism (with its less ancient etymology) came into the English language in the early nineteenth century. It means visiting for pleasure and carries expectations of interest and excitement but not danger and unexpected hazards. Boorstin argues that the nineteenth century was a time when travel declined and tourism replaced it. He writes:

> The traveler ... was working at something; the tourist was a pleasure-seeker. The traveler was active; he went strenuously in search of people, of adventure, of experience. The tourist is passive; he expects interesting things to happen to him. He goes "sightseeing" (a word, by the way, which came in about the same time, with its first use recorded in 1847). He expects everything to be done to him and for him. (1962:85)

This emergence of tourism as the basis for nineteenth- and twentieth-century encounters with other people and places resulted in differences in the quality of that relationship. Tourism became more abbreviated, more insulated, and more secure than the experiences overseas visitors had in earlier centuries. With packaged tours that emerged in the mid-1800s under the direction of Thomas Cook, tourists could be guided gently through these encounters and assisted with the details of getting from port to hotel, changing money, negotiating prices in native markets, deciding what to see, and retreating as needed to unthreatening surroundings.

Since the mid-nineteenth century, this trend has increased so that more and more people visit distant locations. Tourists go with expectations about what they will see and promises that they will actually see them. These expectations are generated, at least in part, by popular cultural representations. Tourists expect to be entertained and to see interesting sights, diversions different enough from those at home to the point of being amusing and providing things to write about on postcards and to tell about in stories. Ideally, the sights should be photogenic and match prior expectations. Again, Boorstin writes:

> The tourist looks for caricature; travel agents at home and national tourist bureaus abroad are quick to oblige. The tourist seldom likes the authentic (to him often unintelligible) product of the foreign culture; he prefers his own provincial expectations. The French chanteuse singing English with a French accent seems more charmingly French than the one who simply sings in French. The American tourist in Japan looks less for what is Japanese than what is Japanesy. (1962:106)

Today tourism is a more common experience than ever before. Once unthinkable, some sort of travel away from home is within reach of the majority of Americans. Even farmers and factory workers can and do visit Europe, the Caribbean, or even more exotic locations. It is not unusual for a college student to spend a term studying in a foreign country. In contemporary business frequent travel is required of many employees. In short, geographic mobility is commonplace in late twentieth-century America.

Instructions in Representing Otherness: Advertisements for Travel Photography

Advertisements for travel photography have promoted the idea of collecting photographic souvenirs in association with domestic and foreign tourism. They have provided specific models to instruct amateur photographers about the composition and content of travel photographs. Just as advertisements helped teach the appropriate moments in a birthday celebration that deserve recording, they have helped standardize cultural expectations about travel photographs.

One of the earliest advertisements of this sort appearing in the *National Geographic* is the 1927 Ciné-Kodak advertisement in Figure 2.2. It encourages the overseas visitor to take movies on board the ocean liner as well as in touristic destinations. By laying out a sequence of different scenes, the advertisement also informs the reader about the home movie camera's narrative possibilities. Additionally, it depicts a social setting back at home in which the tourist, with the help of a home movie, relates to an audience of friends and relatives an account of the trip.

Late twentieth-century retrospective readers of this advertisement must remind themselves that visual images of travel—like visual images in general—were a great deal rarer in 1927 when this advertisement was published. Movies, theaters, and screen stars were all the rage. Members of the public needed encouragement and support to appropriate the world of the silver screen as their own.

The richness of social and cultural information contained in this advertisement is considerable. If Roland Marchand is correct in saying that magazine readers in the 1920s and 1930s tended to linger over advertisements much longer than do contemporary readers, a contemporary reader can imagine some of the things that members of the intended audience may have seen in this advertisement. For example, why is the photographer in the Ciné-Kodak advertisement a woman? Was picture taking generally defined as a feminine task? (Had the depicted photographer been male, it would be relevant to ask, alternatively, why cameras and men were linked.) It is in answering questions like this that the larger discourse of advertisements instead of any single advertisement must be considered. In fact, both men and women are repeatedly portrayed as photographers, and there is no clear shift over time in the gender of the person holding the camera. But there *is* a recurring emphasis in the copy on the simplicity of picture taking and the insistence that any person (even a woman?) can master the skills needed to record travel experiences on film.

"All the world's a movie set when you take along the new 7-speed Filmo 70 D" proclaims another advertisement for travel photography from the late 1920s (Figure 2.3). Only the photographer's feet are visible behind an enlarged and superimposed image of the camera. The reader is privileged with the view not through the lens of the camera but as an onlooker observing the process of photographing. This vantage is an instructional one: the audience for the advertisement sees a model for how to take pictures while traveling abroad. Generic peasants in an unidentified but picturesque village stand ready to dance when the film rolls. The advertisement tells the reader that the Filmo is no toy but a precision instrument that will give the nonprofessional photographer Hollywood-like skills.

Beyond the overt claims about the photographic equipment is the covert depiction of the relationship of the travel photographer to the people visited. They are like actors; they dance to directions. Authority over their lives, their experiences, and their images rests in the hands of the visitor. They are like the camera itself in their functionality as a part of the touristic experience. The frozen scene in the advertisement is but one moment in a larger travel narrative about the relationship of the visitor to the visited. At the bottom of the advertisement, the moral of this story is spelled out: "What you see, you get."

In this advertisement a single moment represents the process of movie taking. The moment selected out of the many possibilities is the one just before the film rolls and the action begins. In the illustration the peasants orient their action to the camera and wait for directions from the photographer. What the film will capture, then, is not an authentic moment in their lives but rather a staged one. This transformation of people's lives—perhaps in moving the dancing into the most photogenic location, where the light and scenery are the best—seems not

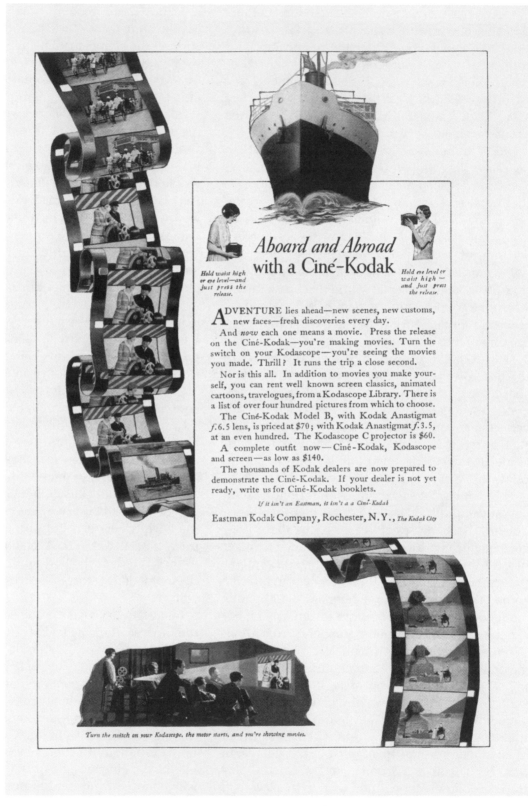

Figure 2.2

All the World's a Movie Set when you take along

THE NEW 7 - SPEED FILMO 70·D

. . . and the skill of an expert Hollywood cameraman is put in your hands by this master of all personal movie cameras—the new Filmo 70 D.

Close-ups, long shots, s-l-o-w motion, *faster* action . . . movies of your travels such as were never known before are at your finger-tips with the seven speeds, three-lens turret, and variable view-finder of this amazing new star in personal moviedom.

A toy? Far from it. An amateur camera? Only in its utter simplicity. Filmo 70 D is a small model of its $5,000 brothers in the professional field. Yet it costs but $245 and up in its May-fair carrying case of English saddle leather, equipped with SESAMEE lock.

Ask your Filmo dealer to demonstrate Filmo 70 D or write us for literature and the illustrated movie booklet, "What you see, you get."

BELL & HOWELL Co., Dept. H, 1817 Larchmont Ave., Chicago, Ill.
New York, Hollywood, London (B. & H. Co. Ltd.) Established 1907

BELL & HOWELL
Filmo
WHAT YOU SEE, YOU GET

Filmo 70 A, the original personal movie camera, surpassed only by Filmo 70 D, $180 and up with carrying case.

Filmo 75, pocket size and aristo-cratic, $120 and up with carrying case.

All Filmos take either a 50 or 100 foot roll of film.

For black and white pictures, Filmo Cameras use Eastman Safety Film (16mm.) in the yellow box—both regular and panchromatic — obtainable at practically all dealers handling cameras and supplies. Filmo Cameras and Filmo Projectors are adaptable, under license from Eastman Kodak Company, for use of Eastman Koda-color film for home movies in full color. Cost of film covers developing and return postpaid, within the country where processed, ready to show at home or anywhere with Filmo Projector.

Figure 2.3

to concern the advertiser or the photographer. The world is, after all, an oyster for the tourist.

A 1930 advertisement for Leica illustrates how a still camera can easily catch " 'camera shy' subjects" (Figure 2.4). Here the subjects are captioned as "Navajo children with their pets." Back at home the tourist can use this photographic souvenir to illustrate a travel account. This photograph has frozen a moment in the flow of images and events that the tourist experienced. The advertisement itself suggests that the narrative that may be told will be about the tourist's preparation for and skill in recording serendipitous moments on film. In this instance the tourist adeptly managed to catch the unsuspecting children off-guard in a candid moment that reveals something that presumably would not be visible in a posed photograph.

Such a narrative also tells the story of the visitor's relation to the visited. Left alone in the advertising copy, perhaps because no answers are really necessary, are such questions as: Do the children want to be photographed? Have their parents given permission? How did the photographer and the photographed interact prior to the moment reflected in the picture? And what will their relationship be afterward? In other words, does the tourist have any responsibility in the relationship with the subjects, or is it merely one of taking pictures *of* them and thus taking *from* them whatever the tourist wants?

The Ciné-Kodak advertisement from 1931 (Figure 2.5) instructs the reader even more fully about how to view the visited both on the spot and in photographically aided recollections. It demonstrates complex relationships of travelers with each other and with those who live in the places visited. As a male photographer takes a picture, his female companion gazes upon the locals. She has assumed a distinctly feminine body cant—bent head, clasped hands, and tilted ankle—and to a late twentieth-century audience hardly seems properly dressed to visit ancient monuments. The copy informs us that these tourists are using the movie camera as "the new way to keep a travel diary."

In the smaller picture, the account they keep in this manner is related to youngsters who see projected upon a screen what the photographer had himself seen through the viewfinder of the camera. The woman did not witness the event from the same angle the filmed account now provides for her; her own genuine experience, seen originally from a different vantage, is therefore replaced by the camera's version of what transpired and how it looked. Its account stands as more authoritative. Even the photographer did not see the actual moment from the exact angle of the camera's lens; his original viewing was framed by the viewfinder and mediated by the camera. In the movie the columns are not so majestic, the activities of the quaintly dressed people emerge as the focus of the account, and the music they played and the tourists once heard is replaced by mime. It is as though the purpose of the trip was less to experience things directly than to construct opportunistically some

The new way to keep a Travel Diary

Make Home Movies as you go — with this $75 Ciné-Kodak

THE CINÉ-KODAK, MODEL M, is the simplest movie camera made, and the lightest that loads with 100 feet of 16 mm. film. Requires no focusing, yet gives you clear, sharp movies. Comes with *f*.3.5 lens and a special attachment for close-ups. Price, with case to match, $75.

THOSE jolly people in Switzerland. Those charming places in Italy. Will they gradually fade in your memory like receding shores from the stern of your home-bound ship? Keep them forever—in movies. Movies that you make yourself with a Ciné-Kodak.

Back home you can enjoy at the flick of your finger all the excitement of your trip abroad.

What a marvelous and easy way to preserve your travels forever.

If you can take a simple snapshot you can easily operate a Ciné-Kodak. All you do is look through a finder and press a lever. It's the simplest of home movie cameras.

At tourists' favorite points abroad you will find Eastman experts ready to finish your Ciné-Kodak films without extra charge.

Stop today at your dealer's and see the Model M. Price $75. Kodascope projectors as low as $60. Many dealers offer an easy payment plan.

Mail coupon for free
HOME MOVIE BOOKLET

Eastman Kodak Company, Rochester, N. Y.
Send me FREE illustrated booklet telling me how I can easily make my own movies.

*Name*_____
*Street*_____
*City*_____*State*_____
                                        H. B. 5

Ciné-Kodak — SIMPLEST OF HOME MOVIE CAMERAS

Figure 2.5

•   25

filmed images that can be experienced at some future time. The images so recorded on film become substitutes for memory and constitute both the structure and content of the travel recollection. It is easy to imagine that the narrative the couple will provide for this silent movie will be about their travel and photographic experiences as well as the people whom they photographed. The movie is their mechanism for telling their children (they do seem undeniably to be husband and wife) about their travels abroad and about their dealings with the local people.

Other questions are not answered in the advertisement: Where were the children while their parents traveled? Did their nanny or some equally affluent relative look after them and keep them happy while their parents were abroad? Or did the parents make the trip before they had children and thus many years before the screening shown in the advertisement?

From this same time period, another Ciné-Kodak advertisement (Figure 2.6) offers further instruction in travel photography. The woman in the picture was photographed (presumably by the man who is her husband) while they were in Egypt. With the aid of the home movies they made, they tell the details of the trip to the older woman who views their movie. She is probably the widowed mother of one member of the couple.

Beyond this outline of their social relationships, further details must be imagined, such as whether the money to travel was inherited or earned, what happened to the older woman's missing husband, and whether this mother had herself once been to Egypt in a time before home movies and is thus reliving her own earlier travel experience. The social relationship between the woman as tourist and the Egyptian with whom she interacts in the movie leaves much less to our imagination. He is showing her his wares, other Egyptians look on, and she is engaged in some stage of an economic interaction with him. Whether she is demonstrating her bargaining skills or her surprise at what he offers for sale it is not possible to say. What is clear is the relationship of the Egyptian as seller and of the American as potential buyer. The balance of power in the

relationship favors her. She may elect to complete the transaction or not, and she can set its terms. The man in the movie depends on her likes and dislikes as well as upon the possibility of her money in exchange for his goods.

Not directly pictured, but nonetheless understood, is the noneconomic relationship of the husband, who was presumably the photographer, to the people visited. There is no indication that the scene is staged and certainly no hint that he has paid those who are the supporting cast in his travel movie for permission to include their images in his film. Retrospectively, this advertisement may represent a more pristine time before natives everywhere began to have set rates for allowing themselves to be photographed. Such alterations of experience came later in the relationship between camera-bearing tourists and those they visited. Again in retrospect, it is possible to imagine this as a pure moment when the traveler merely recorded on film an encounter of his companion with the native people in a distant land. None of the unpleasantness of paying to take pictures or of staged settings seems to occur here.

"Our movies of Mexico cost us less than the tips" (Figure 2.7) may speak to an economy-minded audience in the midst of the depression, but it also iterates the economic inequality between Americans and Mexicans. A more cynical caption for this 1934 Ciné-Kodak advertisement might read, "Affluent Americans visit Mexican peasants." The copy could further explain that the Americans review their vacation during periods of leisure and that the distinction between Mexicans as workers and Americans as vacationers is visually depicted in this home travel movie.

Two themes that recur throughout twentieth-century travel advertisements show the degree to which advertisements for travel photography are a continuous discourse. First, differences between the visitors and the visited are usually emphasized over similarities. This is the case in all the advertisements examined so far. Repetition of difference helps construct otherness. Second, people who live in foreign places are almost always depicted as working. This fact establishes a contrast between

Snap the Switch . . .

and you're back in Egypt

Keep Your Travels in Home Movies with this new $75 Ciné-Kodak

What a thrill! All the vivid details of your journey . . the sights you saw . . people you met . . flashing on the movie screen at home.

There's nothing like home movies to keep travel memories fresh. And there's nothing like a Ciné-Kodak for simplicity.

You look through a finder and press a lever—that's all there is to it.

With equal ease your films are shown. Switch on your Kodascope projector and instantly the screen becomes alive with action.

There, parading before your eyes, are the movies of your

CINÉ-KODAK, MODEL M, *is only $75, with case. Lightest camera made for 100 feet of 16 mm. film.*

travels—movies that you made yourself. People, places, events—real as life, just as you saw them.

At tourists' favorite points abroad, you will find Ciné-Kodak processing stations. There, Eastman experts will finish your Ciné-Kodak films without extra charge.

Your Ciné-Kodak dealer will gladly show you typical movies made with a Ciné-Kodak. And tell you how you can buy a complete outfit on easy terms, if you wish.

Ciné-Kodaks as low as $75. Kodascope projectors as low as $60. Eastman Kodak Company, Rochester, New York.

Ciné-Kodak

SIMPLEST OF HOME MOVIE CAMERAS

Figure 2.6

SOCIETY PLAYS *where Old Hawaiian Kings held court*

THEY roved from beach to coral beach at the royal whim. Sailed in their outrigger canoes in a pagan pageant from the Island of Gardens to the Island Where the Snow Meets the Sky. A simple palace here, in a coco-nut grove of unimaginable beauty and stillness. Another yonder, where one could lie and watch silver flying fish skimming a sea as colorful as the cool depths of an opal.

That was yesterday. Today, to all this native charm is added the modern luxury of world-famous palatial hotels. Smart motors ply the flowered avenues to Waikiki. Gay groups gather on the broad *lanais*. Surfboards and outrigger canoes ride the combers in thrilling races. Life and color and movement everywhere—even at midnight, when the torches of native fishermen sparkle from a distant coral reef.

Summer days are cool for golf, on one of a dozen scenic courses.

Yet winter days are warm in Honolulu's almost changeless climate. Within a few hours' voyage are other fascinating islands—Maui, Hawaii and Kauai—where volcanoes alive and dormant, giant tree fern jungles, shaded tropical gardens, sweeping beaches, deep, iridescent canyons and winding motor roads invite one to weeks of roving.

Stay for it all! Hawaii is only 2,000 miles (four to six days' delightful voyage) from the Pacific Coast; and all-inclusive tours range upward from $400 or $500 including all steamer fares, hotels and sightseeing, for a month's trip with two or three weeks ashore. De luxe accommodations, also, equal to those of Europe's most renowned resorts. Any railroad or travel agent can book you direct from home via San Francisco, Los Angeles, Seattle or Vancouver. No passport formalities—Hawaii is U. S. A.

HAWAII
The WORLD'S *Enchanted Island Playground*

LASSCO LINE from LOS ANGELES

Sailings every Saturday over the delightful Southern route on Lassco luxury liners and popular cabin cruisers. De luxe accommodations; also economy tours on all-expense tickets. Ask at any authorized travel agency or at Los Angeles Steamship Company offices: 730 South Broadway, Los Angeles; 505 Fifth Avenue, New York City; 140 South Dearborn Street, Chicago; 609 Thomas Bldg., Dallas; 685 Market Street, San Francisco; 119 W. Ocean Avenue, Long Beach, Calif.; 217 East Broadway, San Diego, Calif.

MATSON LINE from SAN FRANCISCO

Sailings every Wednesday and every other Saturday over smooth seas on fast de luxe liners; also popular one-class steamers. Novel entertainment features—glorious fun. Attractive all-expense Island tours. Regular sailings also from Seattle and Portland, Ore. See your travel agency or Matson Line: 215 Market Street, San Francisco; 535 Fifth Avenue, New York; 140 South Dearborn Street, Chicago; 1805 Elm Street, Dallas; 723 Seventh Street, Los Angeles; 1319 Fourth Avenue, Seattle; 82½ Fourth Street, Portland, Ore.

HAWAII TOURIST BUREAU
SAN FRANCISCO: P. O. BOX 3615—LOS ANGELES: P. O. BOX 375—HONOLULU, HAWAII: P. O. BOX 2120
Please send me Hawaii booklet in colors and a copy of "Tourfax" travel guide.

55

Name_____ Address_____

Figure 2.7

the tourists who have the leisure and money to travel and those who live in the places that are visited and who must work for their living.

This economic discrepancy between us and them, rich and poor, Americans and "natives" reappears in the Ciné-Kodak advertisement for 1935 showing movie making in Nassau (Figure 2.8). Here the audience comes close to looking right through the viewfinder down upon the natives who are diving for coins tossed from the tourists' ship. The camera angle as well as the photographer's place on board a larger vessel visually communicates the tourist's superiority over the natives.

Whatever the merits of movie cameras to capture action, it is reasonable to ask why grown men are diving from boats to retrieve coins tossed by tourists. Is this merely one of those quaint things natives do, or is there a real economic motive for these men to spend their time retrieving coins cast into the ocean by wealthy tourists? They are adults, but in their relationship to the visitors they are childlike. Like the peasants who dance to the tune played by the amateur movie director in Figure 2.4, these divers orient their lives and economic activities around the actions of others. The inequality of relationships runs throughout the discourse of advertising depicting the experience of tourism. The camera serves to record it.

In scarcely more than half a dozen advertisements, several themes are repeated to the point where particulars fade and consistencies become clear. A tourist brags in a 1940 advertisement that he made some thrilling movies—with a little help from Filmo (Figure 2.9). But what did he take pictures of? The single example selected to illustrate the pride of his accomplishments zeros in on a barefoot worker somewhere in an Asian rice paddy. Work versus leisure; wealth versus poverty; us versus them—these are the recurring themes of home travel movies and the raw materials of personal narratives of travel experiences in the twentieth century.

A 1944 Kodak advertisement (Figure 2.10) lends some credence to the advertisers' claim that advertisements reflect society rather than creating or shaping it. Here is America in time of war. The GI stationed "somewhere in England" has found a surrogate grandmother to whom he proudly shows his snapshots from home. The relationship of the visitor to the visited is different here. This advertisement is about similarity of experience shared across the national boundaries of countries who are allies in war. Common experience and lack of difference are unusual but understandable themes in this special circumstance.

Following the war, the format for the advertising of travel photography established decades earlier reemerges. The technology of home photography continues to change, but the content of relationships does not. Affluent Americans still visit quaint natives who carry baskets or pots on their heads, tend children, and weave or carve. The pictures taken in such circumstances become the basis for a new generation's accounts of travel.

The established code is repeated in the 1957 advertisement for an even more sophisticated camera with three lenses and more film per winding (Figure 2.11). The visited are unaffected by the sophistication of the cameras tourists bring. In the scene about to be photographed, a black youth does one of those quaint native things once again: With bare feet he skillfully climbs a palm tree. This is the stuff of which photographic trophies are constructed. Imagine the delight of the American who can demonstrate photographic prowess back at home. The advertisement suggests that his travel movie will rival those people usually pay to see.

The expansion of the touristic experience among an even greater range of Americans is evident in the 1962 Kodak advertisement (Figure 2.12). Here a family, dressed in western attire, visits the American West. Unlike the children in the 1931 advertisement (Figure 2.5), these children are not left behind but accompany their parents to the tourist destination. In the illustration the process of movie making while traveling is replicated for yet another generation of Americans. The essential aspects of the model—of how to take pictures and what the pictures should show—are unchanged.

Here the entire family observes while Dad films a Native American woman in the Southwest tending her sheep. It is picturesque indeed. The advertise-

Nassau... You're Making Movies with the "K"

● Keep your travel diary this thrilling modern way! Ciné-Kodak "K" absorbs the action, the very life of the places you travel so far to see. Yours for keeps, to throw on the screen in your home as often as you wish. The "K" is so simple to use that the beginner gets excellent movies from his first try—yet its range meets every demand of the expert. Loads with full 100 feet of 16 mm. film. Price, including case, from $112.50. Ask your dealer to show you the "K," and sample movies. Eastman Kodak Company, Rochester, N.Y.... *Only Eastman makes the Kodak.*

Ciné-Kodak 'K'

EASTMAN'S FINEST HOME MOVIE CAMERA

...tra equipment for the ...ncludes four tele-... lenses, for close-...f distant action; the ...-angle lens, giving ...th of view in close ...ers; filters for cloud ...s and scenics; and ...Kodacolor Adjustable ...r for gorgeous movies ...ll natural color.

Figure 2.8

"SURE, I MADE THOSE MOVIES

...but give my Filmo a little credit, too!"

Movie Opportunity No. 390

PALM-SIZE

Filmo 8

MAKES MOVIES
AT SNAPSHOT
COST

ONLY **$49.50**

WHAT a thrill—when your friends praise your personal movies! But the wise movie maker knows that it takes the finest equipment to produce movies that friends compare favorably with Hollywood's product. And he knows that Filmo personal movie cameras and projectors are built by *Bell & Howell*, makers since 1907 of Hollywood's professional equipment.

With a Filmo, it's easy even for beginners to make clear, sparkling, beautiful movies, indoors or out, in full color, too! And with extra speeds including slow motion, device for animating titles, maps, and cartoons, and provision for using telephoto lenses, Filmo is a basic camera which will keep pace with your progress.

Filmos are priced from only $49.50. Your dealer offers easy terms. Mail coupon for free movie booklet. Bell & Howell Company, Chicago; New York; Hollywood; London.

NEW "SHELLOADING"
16 mm.
Filmo

This new 16 mm. Filmo is free from gadgets. It "shelloads" with pre-threaded film magazines. Permits mid-reel changes from color to black-and-white. With fast F 2.7 lens, $115. Other models to $1155.

**FREE
MOVIE
BOOKLET**

BELL & HOWELL COMPANY
1804 Larchmont Ave., Chicago, Ill.
Okay! Send free, 16-page booklet describing:
( ) Palm-size Filmo 8; ( ) new 16 mm. Filmo.

Name...

Address..

City.........................*State*......NG 4-40

PRECISION-MADE BY
BELL & HOWELL

Figure 2.9

• 31

Somewhere in England

It's a proud moment when he can say, "Some new snaps of my folks in the good old U. S."

That American uniform and boyish grin go a long way to open friendly doors, and a fellow, in return, naturally wants to open the door to his own background . . .

He's proud to introduce you to those kindly people—"This is my mother. And this is Dad and Sis in the car—that bus was a honey about five years ago". . .

Give him a chance to show "some new snapshots" and brag about you—he wants to so much. He *needs*, so much, this present link with home.

You may have trouble getting the film—military demands still come first—but when you succeed, be sure to use it taking the scenes closest to his heart—and send the prints just as soon as you can. As far as possible, make your letters "snapshot visits from home". . . Eastman Kodak Co., Rochester, N. Y.

REMEMBER "BLOODY SAIPAN"? How our Marines and Army Infantry fought the costliest battle in Marine Corps history? How the Japs were wiped out after violating the white flag of truce by firing on our men as they approached? . . . This desperate 25-day battle is typical of what our boys must endure—a stern example to us at home. BUY — *HOLD* — MORE WAR BONDS.

Visit your man in the service with SNAPSHOTS

Kodak

Figure 2.10

New Kodak camera gives you the kind of
travel movies people usually *pay* to see!

Cine-Kodak K-100 Turret Camera accommodates Kodak's finest cine lenses . . . runs 40 feet of film with one winding.

This superb new K-100 Turret Camera takes 16mm color movies of theater quality.

With a click of the turret, you can switch to any one of three of the great Kodak Cine Ektar Lenses—standard, telephoto, or wide-angle. Instantly *and automatically* a matching viewfinder frames your scene. And the double-length film run of the K-100 lets you go on shooting while others stop to wind. Camera adapts to make multiple exposures, fades, and dissolves.

See the Cine-Kodak K-100 Turret Camera demonstrated at your photo dealer's now.

With the standard lens: *f*/1.9 Ektar, $315; *f*/1.4, $415. Or pay as little as 10% down. Telephoto and wide-angle lenses and their matching viewfinders are extra. A single-lens model also is available, starting at $279. (*Prices are list, include Federal Tax where applicable, and are subject to change without notice.*)

Another fine Ektar-Lens-equipped camera, this Cine-Kodak Royal Magazine Camera loads in 3 seconds, focuses from 12 inches to horizon. Accepts telephoto and wide-angle lenses. With *f*/1.9 Ektar Lens, $189.50—or $18.95 down.

EASTMAN KODAK COMPANY . . . Rochester 4, N. Y.

Kodak
—*a trade-mark since 1888*

Figure 2.11

• 33

The grandeur comes home wit

How would you describe a magnificent sight like this, once you came back home?

With words alone, it would be difficult. But when you take along a Kodak camera and Kodak film, it's easy to bring back all the beauty and grandeur—*exactly as you saw it.*

This is because all Kodak films are created for *uniform* high quality and *dependable* performance. A good example

is KODACHROME II Film, the new faster better color film for movies and slides.

After Kodak scientists had desi and produced KODACHROME II Film i laboratory, Kodak test-manufactured *three whole years.* We made enoug this film to span the United State was tested in every conceivable light color situation, tried out on mountain

Kodak
—a trade-mark since 1888

ou — in pictures on <u>Kodak</u> film!

ert, exposed to Arctic cold and jungle ..t, measured and rated on every point color quality, stability, consistency, and pendability.

And only when it had met every Kodak ndard—*only when it had proved itself mpletely for three years*—was KODA-ROME II put on the market for you.

But Kodak testing really never ends— KODACHROME II or any other Kodak film. In the daily course of manufacture, all Kodak films are endlessly checked, tested, re-tested, researched, and refined. This is the big reason why you can always depend on Kodak film—any roll, any-where—and on any other product that bears the Kodak name.

EASTMAN KODAK COMPANY
Rochester 4, N. Y.

You can depend on the name Kodak

ment promises high-quality color reproduction to help preserve the experience. Despite ever-continuing technological developments in cameras and film and changes in the vacation habits of the American family, the depiction of others at work while the tourist observes and photographs remains stable.

Although the 1963 advertisement by the Government of India Tourist Office (Figure 2.13) is not an advertisement for photographic equipment, it does instruct its audience about the role of photography in travel. Perched atop an elephant in Jaipur and about to take one of the more unusual rides of his life, the American tourist actively records the experience with his camera. A moment's reflection, however, reveals that the picture the man is taking will not show him and his female companion on the elephant; rather, it will show what he saw from atop the elephant. This advertisement thus teases us about the photographic souvenir that will result. The tourist's narrative back at home may very well include some apology for not having the best picture of all: of what they looked like on the elephant's back. In any case it appears that the tourist's behavior in this advertisement conforms to earlier advertising models of the relation among the tourist, the camera, and the visited.

"Okay, get the camera! This is a Kodak moment" is a commonplace way for many Americans to signal the assessment of a situation as worthy of photographing. For more than twenty years, Kodak has been demonstrating such moments in its advertising. "Would you risk this moment on anything less than Kodak film?" asks a 1972 advertisement (Figure 2.14). If it's worth saving, Kodak wants Americans to believe, it's worth using Kodak film. But what are these moments? The 1972 advertisement appearing in *Life* magazine illustrates one. No words were necessary to demonstrate the excitement of twin boys sitting in the lap of an Indian chief. A charming moment worth remembering. A moment about children, fantasies, adventure—and otherness. This particular Kodak moment is made out of the difference between the boys and the man, of their being able to pretend to be brave and fearless Indian chiefs, and of their having "been there and done

that." It is of course possible that these boys might sit in the lap of a postman and dress up with mail carrier hats or in Santa's lap with red caps with white fur. But this is one of those moments in representing *other* people and their lives. What is interesting about the Indian chief is his difference and exoticism, not his similarity to *Life*'s audience of largely white readers.

By midcentury, advertising had helped to secure a place for the camera in the hand baggage of nearly every tourist. More recent advertisements for travel photography repeat the essential themes that were laid down in earlier decades of the twentieth century. The advertisements continue to report on newer photographic technologies and encourage their purchase. Travel itself becomes more common across social classes in America. The Egyptian pyramids, the Eiffel Tower, and Big Ben continue as recommended subjects for photographs in advertisements.

Today the concept of tourism is widely understood by Americans. It bears little relationship to the travel experiences of earlier times that Boorstin describes. As tourism has become widespread, the public has come to share a conception of what to do and what to expect as tourists. The camera is so much a part of that experience that the sight of one dangling around a person's neck almost ensures that he or she will be imagined to be a tourist. Advertisements have not only taught the American public technical details about cameras and film, but they have provided important models for picture taking. These instructions have offered patterns for the contents of travel pictures and have explained the process of taking them. But they have also spelled out a secondary message about the relationship between the visitors and the visited. These models have explained who is rich and who is poor. They have documented who has leisure and who must work. They have explained the differences between our lives and theirs. They have reminded us of who we are and how other people differ from us. They have not told us a story of common humanity but of fundamental economic, political, and cultural differences.

Sitting pretty in the Pink City

This is the way to see Jaipur—from a golden howdah atop a painted elephant.

From New York, you can take a jet to Delhi, an air-conditioned train or chauffeur-driven car to Jaipur, but once in Jaipur, choose a maharajah's palace for your hotel, and an elephant to see the sights. Just as his ancestors have borne Rajput princes, so will "Hathi" take you up the winding hillside road to Fort Amber.

You will literally see the world below through rose-colored glasses. For all Jaipur is sculptured from soft pink sandstone. Visitors affectionately call it the Pink City. Architects call it the most beautiful city in the world. Its people will recount to you romantic tales of chivalry of the proud Rajputs who chose to die in defense of their honor.

When you can bring yourself to leave Jaipur, fly south to Udaipur with its floating palaces, to Mount Abu with its marble temples, south to cosmopolitan Bombay.

For brochure on Jaipur see your travel agent or write

Government of

India

Tourist Office

NEW YORK: 19 East 49th Street

SAN FRANCISCO: 685 Market Street

TORONTO: 177 King Street W.

Come to Jaipur. Sooner or later most world travellers do.

Figure 2.13

Would you risk this moment o

anything less than Kodak film?

Kodak makes your
pictures count.

In two remaining sections of this chapter, I look at evidence from sources outside the discourse of advertising that support this interpretation of the secondary discourse in travel photography advertisements. The sources I examine are travel photography manuals and some remarks about photography made by the professional photographer Margaret Bourke-White. These sources put more explicitly into words the themes found within the advertisements.

Travel Photography Manuals: Explaining the Ideology of Photographic Colonialism

Since the introduction of cameras for nonprofessional photographers, Kodak, Bell and Howell, and other manufacturing companies as well as individual experts on photography have published manuals giving the public advice on picture taking. These handbooks, like the advertisements just considered, contain information about both the technical aspects of photography and the place of cameras and photographs in society and culture. Their instructions on travel photography are of special interest because they deal with the representation of other people.

Although most general manuals contain some advice on travel photography, a few are devoted entirely to this subject. One of the more comprehensive is *How to Take Better Travel Photos,* written by Lisl Dennis in 1979. Dennis, a freelance photographer based in New York City, specializes in travel photography. In one of the nine sections of her 160-page book, she discusses issues concerning people. Some of the advice is technical in nature, but most of it focuses on what the pictures should contain and how to deal with those who are being photographed.

Dennis illustrates the results of the techniques she recommends by including some engaging portraits of people from the many countries she has visited. The quality of these pictures demonstrates why her photographs have appeared in numerous

American and foreign magazines as well as in travel advertisements and promotional brochures.

Her manual can also be given a critical reading for what it has to say on the relationship between the photographer and the photographed and for its instructions on how the visitor should deal with the visited. Such a reading requires shifting attention from the overt discussion in the text to a consideration of more covert issues that echo many of the instructions contained in travel photography advertisements. However, this text differs from the advertisements in the explicitness of its instructions and the ideology on which they are predicated.

Dennis's chapter on people in travel photography begins with an account of how she managed to capture just the right expression in a close-up portrait of a boy in the French West Indies:

One languid day in the French West Indies, I took a stroll with my camera and 55mm lens. I soon came upon a little boy sitting in the doorway of his home. We stared at each other, and I thought he had a rather beguiling face. …

I gingerly walked into the yard to get permission from the boy's mother to take his picture. Marching into someone's property is always risky, so do it with caution. … Neither the boy's mother or any dogs seemed to be at home.

I gave the child a body-language greeting because I don't speak French well. A gentle wave of the hand and a wide smile work in all cultures. He didn't appear to be at all apprehensive, so I smiled even more and slowly raised the camera to my eye to make a couple of preliminary, ice-breaker exposures. I knew from the start I wanted to get a close-up of the boy's face, but I didn't yet know how close I could eventually get.

My first shots were of the boy seated in the doorway. He was still posing unflinchingly after these, so I moved in closer for a head-and-shoulder portrait. …

Knowing the child felt perfectly comfortable with me, I took a few of the strips [of plastic covering the doorway] and rearranged them in his hands and around his face. Immediately he got the message to hold onto them while I zeroed in with the macro lens about four inches from his nose. He loved it, so did I, and so did Mom. At the end of the shooting I looked up and saw her leaning out of a window. She'd been watching all the while! (1979:64–65)

This text, and other similar material in the chapter, can be read either as advice on how to obtain impressive portraits of people living in touristic destinations or as a text detailing the manipulation of other people in the quest for photographic souvenirs. Read in the first manner, this description of photographic aggressiveness seems relatively benign, even adventuresome. Read in the second, it is about exploitation of others to satisfy one's own desires.

This second reading is not a comforting interpretation. The account then becomes not merely a text about using others to fulfill the visitor's wishes but using children in doing so. Moreover, we learn from her own report that Dennis had the intention to ask the child's mother for permission. When she found neither the mother nor dogs to ward her off, she proceeded anyway. We do learn in the end that the child's mother apparently knew and approved of the photographic encounter, but Dennis learned this only after the fact. She had photographed the child without it. This account, written long afterward, gives no hint whatsoever that had the mother never appeared, Dennis would have sought her permission in some way. The image of the child, once acquired by the photographer, apparently becomes the property of the photographer. It is a kind of booty, a souvenir of exploration, a thing captured somewhere else that becomes the property of the one who does the capturing.

No matter how innocent Dennis may think her motives are, what she describes here is *photographic colonialism*. The similarities to economic and political colonialism are remarkable. We are instructed in this manual that the people who live in other parts of the world are the raw materials for our photographs. Since they are neither using their own images nor seem to care or object, we may appropriate them. Back at home, we turn them into souvenirs for display or even products that can be sold. Once the pictures are taken from the indigenous setting, we seem to have no further responsibility to those whose lives supplied the images for our photographs.

Two additional themes in the chapter confirm this interpretation. In a section entitled "Controlling Travel Portraits," Dennis offers advice on dealing with reluctant subjects. She gives tips on catching those who, jaded by their relationships with previous photographers, "pose and run" before a shooting session is finished. She explains how coaxing and maneuvering people into photogenic settings can produce perfectly composed photographs. These manipulations are not considered distortions of the cultures represented. Cooperative and patient subjects are said to provide relief from such effort, but even with them techniques of management are needed to produce excellent pictures.

In the section "To Tip or Not to Tip?" Dennis deals with the uncomfortable (for her) matter of whether any kind of payment is due to the subjects she photographs. Her advice on this matter begins with an anecdote:

Recently I reintroduced myself to a woman with whom I'd traveled in Haiti on a press trip. She'd been with her husband, a prominent travel writer.

"Oh, yes, I remember you," she said. "You're the photographer who never gave that poor person in Haiti any money after you took her picture." Yes, that was me.

This woman with the flawless memory was dragging up ancient history. The incident must have impressed her because it was about three years ago. We had shared a car and stopped to do some shooting. I saw a Haitian lady walking down a road, balancing a huge basket on her head.

I approached her in a cheery fashion as one human being glad to meet another. My dark-skinned sister didn't mind my taking her photograph after I asked her permission. I made about six exposures, and I shook her hand afterwards with smiles and warm thanks. She was giggling and pleased by my attention. However, she requested no financial recompense and seemed satisfied with the personal interaction of the shooting.

Queued behind me to take pictures of the same woman was the prominent travel writer. He made one perfunctory exposure and never made eye contact with the Haitian. Then he nervously slipped a dollar out of his wallet and gave it to the woman. There was no human touch—only payoff.

One American dollar would probably take two days of hard work to earn in Haiti. This local lady had earned one in less than one second. I'm sure no photographer will ever get a picture of her again for anything less than a dollar. Furthermore, she probably waved that greenback all over her village, and now all its denizens might have a $1.00 minimum price for photo privileges. Possibly an entire village of Haitians was turned into *photo-extortionists* by a single insensitive and self-justifying American assuaging his self-image by throwing around money.

This anecdote discloses my general feelings about tipping for photography in foreign lands. (Dennis 1977:74, emphasis added)

In this complex section of her chapter, Dennis echoes a sentiment similar to the advertisement in Figure 2.3. Her attitude in dealing with the Haitian woman reminds us of the idea that "all the world's a movie set." Seen from such a perspective, the quaintness of other people's lives exists, at least in part, as subject matter for the tourist's photographs.

If this story were told without the final two paragraphs, we would draw a very different impression of the underlying attitudes. However, Dennis denies the woman's right to profit from the sale of her image. She even considers that the other photographer's payment encourages what she terms photo-extortion. This kind of language is used elsewhere to dissociate us from the political objectives of others with whom we disagree. For example, when "terrorists" demand ransom from Western nations, it is termed extortion. But when the U.S. government makes demands on other governments with whom it disagrees and from whom it might withhold foreign aid, Washington never employs such language in describing its own behavior.

Dennis is not alone in expressing this attitude toward exchanging money with the visited for the purpose of photographing them. She argues that there are things people consider more valuable than money. Money has its place, and she admits that she has sometimes tipped when the occasion seemed right. For instance, she reports that she once prevailed upon a little boy in St. Lucia to pose for her for over half an hour, which prevented him from selling souvenirs to other tourists. Although the child asked for no money, she gave him some change. She claims that "it felt right" in this instance (77).

A preferred alternative to money is sending the person a print of the picture—a recommendation she makes to her readers. She urges photographers to carry a pencil and a notebook to take down names and addresses. But she admits that she has not always followed through on her promises: "It is sometimes expensive after you add the costs of film, prints and postage" (78).

We might well ask whether this is not further evidence of an exploitative relationship between the photographer and the photographed. Dennis thinks not. She argues that selecting people as subjects is often flattering and that photographing them can "do something positive for their self-esteem" (79). She urges hearty expressions of appreciation to subjects and suspects that "it will also do more for international and interpersonal relations than throwing money around" (79).

Thus, a travel photography manual can be read—as we have read advertisements for travel photography—for the ideology it expresses. This is not its overt message but a secondary message that lies beneath the surface. Whether we find such an interpretation comfortable or pleasing, we must not stop at a superficial, noncritical reading of either the advertisements or manuals that would be limited to discussions of equipment and technique. We must look deeper for the social relationships that are described in both texts. These relationships posit a hierarchical structure of society in which only some of the people make decisions, only some of the people are wealthy, and only some of the people must work. These texts are ideological treatises that explain the nature of things to their audiences.

Photography and Ideology: Margaret Bourke-White in Russia

Another context where these issues of interpreting advertisements for travel photography is made more explicit is the writings and speeches of travel photographers. These texts sometimes bring the ideological premises and objectives sharply into focus. I turn now to consider such an instance where a well-known documentary photographer, Margaret Bourke-White, commented on the ideological aspects of her photography. Like the manuals on travel photography, this text raises more overtly the sorts of issues I have examined in the advertisements for travel photography.

In the early 1930s, the J. Walter Thompson advertising agency held meetings in its New York office for members of its creative staff. It was the company's custom to have an employee or someone else address topics of concern to the advertising business. Verbatim transcripts of many of these meetings survive and give us a window on some of the issues that concerned advertising agency personnel in this period when photography and advertising were becoming intertwined.

On February 1, 1933, Margaret Bourke-White, who was by then established as a premier American photographer and photojournalist, addressed the meeting. Her topic was a review of her work in America and abroad. In particular, she addressed two of the subjects she had photographed in her career: steel mills in the United States and life in Russia. She was already famous for her photographs of American industry, and she had recently returned from a trip to Russia, where she had finally gained permission to photograph Soviet industry, schools, cultural institutions, and the countryside. The presentation was richly illustrated by Bourke-White's photographs.

Her remarks were intended to show the complexity and artistry of photography to the creative staff who were just beginning to use photographs seriously in their advertisements. Indeed, Helen Resor, one of the directors of the company, expressed the opinion that she hoped a better understanding of Bourke-White's techniques and ideas would allow photography to be used to greater advantage in the advertisements produced by the J. Walter Thompson Company.

In her description of her photographs of molten steel, Bourke-White remarked about the difficulties of capturing the process on film. The rapid cooling of the steel is associated with parallel changes in its color and the light it gives off. The extreme heat inside the mill causes camera malfunction and requires ingenious techniques. Other difficulties included getting permission to take the pictures in the first place, but once she had secured it, she took it as carte blanche and proceeded apace to experiment with the representation of steelmaking in her photographs.

This description of industrial production in America stands in marked contrast to her description of life in the Soviet Union. Although she chose some parallel subjects, such as factories, the subject matter became the oddity of differences. Soviet workers, unaccustomed to the machines, tended to stand around and look at them. The social order of the factory occasioned commentary: The boss could not dismiss workers, but workers could and did sometimes dismiss bosses.

Nowhere is the difference between American and Soviet life more apparent than in her remarks about schools:

> To understand Russia you must understand that the Russian government is doing a huge selling job. It doesn't correspond to our selling jobs here, but it can certainly be called advertising. There is no private trade in Russia. The Soviet State is selling the idea of Communism instead of religion, socialism instead of capitalism. It is selling the idea of collective instead of individual work. It is interesting to see how that has worked out in school. The Soviet State is turning particular attention toward the early training of children. In the early days of the new regime the children were never allowed to play with one toy alone. They had a ball so large that it took five children to play with it and a toy locomotive so large that half a dozen children played with it at once. In the colleges one student was never allowed to work out a mathematical problem alone. Several students worked it out together.

What is most notable about this description is its focus on differences. Bourke-White's photographs of America were celebrations of industry and capitalist productivity; they were not about the drudgery of line work and of the excessive heat in steel mills as they affected those who worked in them. Her photographs of Russia were also ideological treatises. The subject matter here was collectivism and other differences from the United States; she seems not to have sought out commonalities and shared patterns in the lives of people living under very different political and economic systems.

Thus, we find in Bourke-White's account of her craft and artistry the lens of ideology through which her subject matter is filtered. Only some things can become the subject of the photographs we take. It is not the inherent interest of the subject matter that attracts us so much as it is the opportunity to express in photographs the social patterns and cultural values that govern our lives.

Bourke-White's remarks articulate some of the thoughts of a professional photographer. For the most part, she has always kept her commentary brief and tended to let her photographs speak for themselves. However, if we learn to listen to her words and to look carefully at her photographs for more than their aesthetics, we come to understand the significance of her choices of subjects and how she chose to represent them. In this succinct way, we see again how representations of other people's lives reflect, shape, and even construct our conceptions of them.

Bibliographic Notes

The *National Geographic* magazine was selected more or less by accident. On a lengthy trip through the Canadian maritime provinces a few years ago, I took to stopping at the many yard sales along the rural roads. Practically the only printed materials that were offered for sale were old issues of the *Geographic*. I bought some of them for summertime reading but soon came to realize that the sellers were parting with magazines that they had been saving for years. Many of the issues were well worn, suggesting that the articles and visual images—including the advertisements—had been seen many times. Thus, I reckoned this was as good a source as any, and perhaps better than more ephemeral ones, to use in studying the instructions that advertisements provided regarding photography and travel.

The Kodak print collection, from which some of the advertisements in this chapter were drawn, is a part of the J. Walter Thompson Company Archives housed in the Special Collections Department of Perkins Library, Duke University. The print collection begins in 1930, the year Thompson got the Kodak account. The earlier advertisement reprinted as Figure 2.2 was provided by the Kodak Company from its collection.

Readers interested in the evolution of the camera will find Reese Jenkins's *Images and Enterprise: Technology and the American Photographic Industry, 1839 to 1925* (Baltimore: Johns Hopkins University Press, 1975) a helpful introduction. Other useful sources on photography and photographic history are Ian Jeffrey's *Photography: A Concise History* (New York: Oxford University Press, 1981) and Susan Sontag's *On Photography* (New York: Farrar, Straus, and Giroux, 1977). Richard Chalfen's *Snapshot Versions of Life* (Bowling Green, Ohio: Bowling Green State University Popular Press, 1987) provides a good overview of nonprofessional uses of cameras. Pierre Bordieu, in *Photography: A Middle-brow Art,* trans. Shaun Whiteside (Stanford: Stanford University Press, 1990), places everyday photography in its social and cultural context by examining the ways in which people use their cameras and the manner in which these uses are socially patterned.

Daniel Boorstin's comments on photography are to be found in his essay "From Traveler to Tourist: The Lost Art of Travel," which is chapter 3 of his book *The Image: A Guide to Pseudo-events in America* (New York: Atheneum, 1973). In addition to Boorstin, other useful sources on travel and tourism are Jonathan Culler, "The Semiotics of Tourism," *American Journal of Semiotics* 1, 1-2 (1981), 127–140; Valene Smith, ed., *Hosts and Guests: The Anthropology of Tourism* (Philadelphia: University of Pennsylvania Press, 1989) and *The Anthropology of Tourism* (New York: Pergamon, 1983), a special issue of *Annals of Tourism Research* 10, 1, edited by Nelson H. H. Graburn.

Margaret Bourke-White is an especially well known figure in the history of photography. In addition to the many books of her photographs, an even greater number of books about them have been published. Her remarks to the J. Walter Thompson Company on February 1, 1933, which are quoted in this chapter, are to be found in the Special Collections Department of Perkins Library, Duke University. In addition, she discussed her experiences in and views on Russia in a series on the Soviet Union that appeared in the *New York Times Magazine,* February 14, 1932, March 6, 13, and 27, 1932; May 22, 1932; and September 11, 1932.

3

Representations of Others, Part 1

Advertisements in the 1929 *National Geographic* Magazine

BENEATH MESSAGES promoting goods and services flow complex images of otherness. This secondary discourse depicts some of our culture's most pervasive ideas about other people and the circumstances of their lives. These images help construct for their intended audience ideas about those who are defined as outside that audience. In addition to the images of other people and their cultures that appear in advertisements for travel to other countries, a remarkable number appear in situations where the imagery of other cultures is borrowed to make selling pitches for products quite unrelated to the people and/or cultures depicted.

For example, the advertisement in Figure 3.1 promotes the Grebe Synchrophase radio, in combination with the Grebe "natural speaker," to American readers of the *National Geographic* in the 1920s. A drawing of an African drummer appears in the advertisement. Through the explanation provided beneath the drawing, the reader learns about the pitch, clarity, and speed of African drum communication but must make the link that the Grebe natural speaker has these same characteristics. These aspects of drum communication in Africa are appropriated from their distant context and suggested as raw materials for the reader to use in developing an understanding of the qualities of the radio and speakers. These matters concern the primary business of the advertisement—selling the Grebe Synchrophase radio over the competition on the basis of its superior characteristics.

But there is more. Also present in the advertise-ment are the materials for developing other ideas. These include but are not limited to such things as differences between modern and primitive technology, virtual nakedness versus Western conventions of clothing, houses constructed from trees and grasses versus wood and stone, primitive versus civilized, and so on. In addition to drawing inferences about the advertised product, what is to stop the reader from drawing inferences about other peoples and cultures as well? This process of borrowing references from sources external to advertising is what Judith Williamson had in mind in her discussion of *referent systems* in *Decoding Advertisements*. Such external references are not merely borrowed in advertisements to make selling points. Indeed that happens, but in addition the understanding of the external referents may be transformed by the borrowing process. Advertising is really unconcerned with original meaning of the referents appropriated for such purposes. In this instance, African drum communication is decontextualized. This is an advertisement for radios and speakers, not some anthropological study of African culture or indigenous processes of communication. The reader never learns what drum communication means in its original context, only that some aspects of it are similar to the standards of tone that Grebe has for its radio and speakers.

This is the first of two chapters in which I examine the representations of other people and cultures in the discourse of American advertising. It would be nearly impossible to undertake a study of

Transmitting messages with his drum, the African depends on the pitch and clarity of its tone. With amazing speed these messages are sent over miles of mountains and jungle.

TONE—Full, deep, resonant—unequaled in its naturalness. As the music is played, as the artist sings, so you should hear it—true, rich, life-like—so faithfully reproduced that you forget you are listening to radio.

This is what you enjoy with a Grebe Synchrophase Seven, particularly in combination with the Grebe Natural Speaker: A tone quality that is unrivaled for its naturalness, an ease of operation that is remarkable for its simplicity, and a refinement of appearance that harmonizes with any environment. Grebe Synchrophase Seven, $135; Grebe Natural Speaker, $35. Send for Booklet N; then ask your dealer to demonstrate.

The GREBE SYNCHROPHASE RADIO

A. H. Grebe & Company, Inc., 109 West 57th Street, New York City
Factory: Richmond Hill, N. Y.   Western Branch: 443 S. San Pedro St., Los Angeles, Cal.
The oldest exclusive radio manufacturer

Figure 3.1

all such images within twentieth-century advertising. The volume of print advertisements alone is truly staggering. Moreover, the advertisements have been poorly preserved and are not easily accessible. The newspapers and popular magazines in which they were printed were intended to be thrown away. Even research libraries that subscribe to nonscholarly publications frequently discard tattered originals in favor of more durable microfilm copies. Advertisements appearing on posters and billboards were often destroyed by the elements before they were intentionally replaced. Nor have radio and television commercials fared much better. There is no systematic archival collection of these commercial messages, which often "evaporate" as soon as they are broadcast. Thus, the discourse of advertising appears in fragile media, but it leaves strong afterimages nonetheless.

Quite remarkably, the scholars who have focused on the content of this discourse have had relatively little to say about the representation of other peoples and their cultures. Although elaborate sampling schemes could be devised to survey the incidence and content of images of otherness in American advertising, such effort is unnecessary to comprehend the ideology that advertising has constructed about other people. A few magazines from the shelves of a resale shop or some recent ones still sitting around the house will do, and even an hour of television watched with the mindset of trying to distance oneself from the familiar can bring this issue squarely to attention. What is opened thereby, perhaps for the first time in a conscious and investigatory manner, are the representations of other people in the abundance of advertisements. This exercise might even result in the conclusion that advertising's discourse about otherness is at least as significant in shaping ideas as formal lessons in geography, world history, and anthropology.

In this chapter I examine in some detail the first of two different historical moments in the discourse. Although I give reasons for selecting these points in time, others would do just as well. What is to be seen through any such window is a set of ideas and issues associated with otherness that is conditioned by the historical circumstances within which the representation occurs. Times of peace and war have occasioned different images, as do other changes in the political, economic, and cultural relationships with the depicted people. Cultures are brought into or banished from the discourse of advertising on such bases. As long as the conditioning of historical circumstances is kept in mind, the representational process itself and the general lessons it contains about otherness will be understandable.

A Window on Otherness: The *National Geographic* Magazine in 1929

In this chapter I look at images of otherness in American advertising just prior to the Great Depression. The twelve issues of the *National Geographic* magazine that appeared in 1929 are my window onto this first historical moment. More than one thousand advertisements appeared in them, but I am able to examine only a few critically. However, what this exercise teaches can be the basis for examining other publications and different periods.

The National Geographic Society was organized in 1888 as an all-male social club in Washington, D.C., for the stated purpose of promoting geographic knowledge. It has grown from such staid beginnings into the world's largest scientific organization as well as one of the world's largest and most profitable publishers. Its primary publication, the *National Geographic* magazine, is currently the third most widely circulating magazine in the United States after *Reader's Digest* and *TV Guide*.

The first issue, published in October 1888, was slim and dull by contemporary standards and included only technical articles on scientific aspects of geography. Within a few years the *National Geographic* became immensely popular nationally and internationally under the leadership of Alexander Graham Bell and his son-in-law, Gilbert Hovey Grosvenor. The initial secret of success was Grosvenor's effort to imitate the great classics in ge-

ography. After studying the accounts of Herodi-
tus, Charles Darwin, and other explorers, he determined that "each one was an articulate, eyewit-
ness, first-hand account. Each contained simple,
straightforward writing—writing that sought to
make pictures in the mind" (Grosvenor 1957:23–24).
He articulated seven principles that are still maintained as guidelines: (1) absolute accuracy; (2) an
abundance of beautiful, instructive, and artistic illustrations; (3) the permanent value of everything
printed; (4) avoidance of all personalities and notes
of a trivial character; (5) avoidance of any partisan
or controversial matters; (6) only favorable commentary about any country or people; and (7)
timely content.

Only members of the society receive the *National
Geographic*. Unlike most other magazines, this one
tends to be saved. The well-preserved issues for
sale at used-book stores, thrift shops, and yard
sales indicate just how long it seems to take many
people to part with the *National Geographic*.
Speaking at the inauguration of the society's new
building in Washington in 1984, President Ronald
Reagan mentioned this tendency to save the magazine; he joked that it was clear to him why the society had to move into new space, since he and his
wife had also faced the problem of what to do with
their collection of the *National Geographic* when
they moved from California to Washington.

The sentiment behind Reagan's remarks and the
widespread practice of keeping the magazine is a
major reason why I use it as a window on the discourse of advertising in the late 1920s. Although the
primary text of the *National Geographic* focuses on
people and places around the world, the advertisements published in the magazine—and saved
along with the articles—constitute a second text
about many of these same people and places.

Although there is no good evidence about how
much attention readers of the magazine paid to the
advertisements appearing at the front and back of
(but never interspersed with) the articles, I surmise
that these advertisements received at least as much
attention as any. Thus, I examine these advertisements for what they reveal about other people and

cultures represented in the discourse of advertising
in the late 1920s.

The Broader Context:
The State of the World in 1929

One might never know it from reading the articles
and advertisements that appeared in the 1929 issues of the *National Geographic*, but there was considerable turmoil in the affairs of the world that
year. In January Leon Trotsky was exiled from the
Soviet Union. In February Benito Mussolini signed
the Lateran treaty that established the Vatican as a
city-state with the pope as its temporal ruler. In
Chicago that same month, six gangsters were killed
in the St. Valentine's Day massacre. In March student riots in Spain led to the closing of Madrid University. In April Joseph Stalin's First Five-Year Plan
established production goals for the Soviet Union;
the brutal means used to implement them resulted
in the deaths of an estimated 5 million people. In
May the United States Supreme Court upheld a
lower court's denial of citizenship to Rosika
Schwimmer, a Hungarian immigrant who was an
avowed pacifist. In July quotas went into effect that
restricted free immigration into the United States.
In August Palestinian Arabs attacked Jews praying
at the Wailing Wall of the ancient temple in Jerusa-
lem. In October the stock market experienced its
greatest single-day loss. In December fighting between Muslims and Hindus in India intensified.

This chronicle of some major newsmaking
events in 1929 portrays a world quite different from
the one depicted in the articles and advertisements
appearing in the *National Geographic* that same
year. By contrast to world events, the magazine's articles dealt with such topics as the volcanoes of Ecuador, school life in Turkey, bypaths of Spain,
Thomas Jefferson's Monticello, drought in East Africa, the English Lake District, a seaplane adventure
in Papua, and Alpine villagers of Austria. The advertisements were equally removed from political,
economic, and ethnic strife in the world. They promoted automobiles, cameras, radios, insurance,
travel, and the like. And they did so in a detached,

romantic, and upbeat manner that emphasized the goods and services in their most positive ways. Seen in this light, the advertisements hardly seem to be reflections of society and culture. Rather, they constitute limited and specialized representations, even fantasies, of the people and cultures depicted in them.

The analytic paradigm proposed in Chapter 1 is useful in this investigation. First, I examine the social categories of others that are constructed in the advertisements, paying particular attention to depictions of the native peoples of North America and South Africa. Second, I study the relationship between the members of the intended audience (whom I assume to be the literate and well-to-do subscribers of the *National Geographic* magazine) to those who are defined as outside it (by lack of any evidence of their inclusion). Third, I look at the nature of the proposed relationships, especially the degree to which they are egalitarian or not.

Native Americans

The 1929 *National Geographic* contains many advertisements promoting travel through, and sometimes to, the American West. No less than five different railway companies advertise such services. In the process they also portray, and thus construct, an image of the American West and especially of the Native Americans who live there.

Southern Pacific advertises travel to California through "Apacheland" (Figure 3.2). The predominant visual imagery is a band of ferocious Indians, armed with rifles, astride swift horses looking as authentic as those on any movie set. The advertisement's theme of the Southwest as a "land of contrasts" is communicated visually by a smaller drawing of the Roosevelt Dam that appears below the picture of the Indians. The caption proclaims that the dam, located on the Apache Trail, "stores life and wealth for the desert." The copy describes the three civilizations that have flourished in southern Arizona: the Apache, "once made famous by Chief Geronimo"; an ancient but extinct people "who dwelt in cliff houses—and who vanished for no

known reason, perhaps a thousand years before Coronado's mailed Spaniards rode by"; and modern southern Arizona, land of "huge copper mines, the mighty Roosevelt Dam and Lake, and the astonishing green agriculture of the Salt River Valley."

The Apache warriors are mythologized in the advertising copy: "Down from their passes in Geronimo's day swept the hard-riding savages to wreak ruin and torture upon the settlers beneath. When finally overwhelmed by white men's armies, fifty years ago, they asked only to be allowed to go back into the mountains they loved—to those peaks that look so relentless, yet cast such a spell upon all who come their way."

This image of the Native American depicted in picture and word is that of the cowboy-and-Indian movie. The advertisement admits that times have changed, but it nonetheless preserves anachronistically the conflict of cultures on the American frontier. The reader is encouraged to believe that the Apache, although conquered and subdued, are not reservation Indians but authentic and genuine examples of the exotic living within the borders of the United States. Moreover, the advertisement proclaims, they can be safely visited five times a day by trains from the East en route to California.

The Rock Island Line (Figure 3.3) offers its travel through the land of the "weirdly beautiful" Apache Trail to California "across the first page of American history." Unlike the Southern Pacific advertisement's outright denigration of the Indian as savage, the Rock Island promotion describes the Southwest as a land "where history was in the making when Rome was 'Growing up to Might'—pre-historic cliff-dwellings and ruined temples, old as the Coliseum—thoroughfares, time-worn as the Appian Way." This is one of the few characterizations of Native Americans in which the Indians are compared favorably to Anglos. But note that the comparison is to extinct Native American cultures, not contemporary or recent ones.

Contemporaneous native culture is the subject of the Santa Fe System's 1929 advertisements (Figures 3.4 and 3.5). This company, which often uses the profile of an Indian chief and other Native American symbols in its logo, urges its customers to take

Thru Apacheland to California

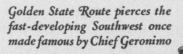

Golden State Route pierces the fast-developing Southwest once made famous by Chief Geronimo

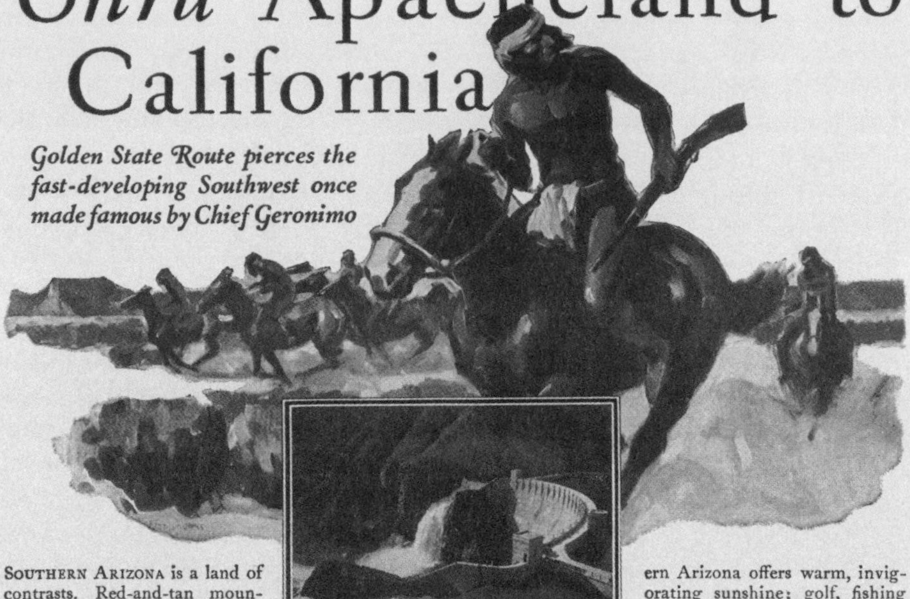

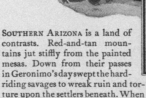

The mighty Roosevelt Dam, on the Apache Trail, stores life and wealth for the desert

SOUTHERN ARIZONA is a land of contrasts. Red-and-tan mountains jut stiffly from the painted mesas. Down from their passes in Geronimo's day swept the hard-riding savages to wreak ruin and torture upon the settlers beneath. When finally overwhelmed by white men's armies, fifty years ago, they asked only to be allowed to go back into the mountains they loved—to those peaks that look so relentless, yet cast such a spell upon all who come their way.

And the land of the Apaches has nourished two other civilizations—one very old and the other very new. Once it cradled a people who dwelt in cliff houses—and who vanished, for no known reason, perhaps a thousand years before Coronado's mailed Spaniards rode by. You can see their dwellings still, as you travel through Apacheland

Today huge copper mines, the mighty Roosevelt Dam and Lake, and the astonishing green agriculture of the Salt River Valley about Phoenix give vitality and wealth to this countryside where once the settler dwelt in grim hardship, his rifle ever at his saddle-bow.

See southern Arizona! It is one of the most fascinating lands on earth. From October to June it is at its best, with picturesque guest ranches open to the visitor, and delightful new, modern tourist hotels at Tucson, Chandler and Phoenix. Southern Arizona offers warm, invigorating sunshine; golf, fishing and big-game hunting; and many a historic shrine to visit.

Southern Pacific's GOLDEN STATE and SUNSET ROUTES serve the spirited region. Five trains daily for California pass right through the heart of the old Apache and modern guest-ranch country, and the winter desert resorts of southern California. Visit it on your way to the Pacific Coast. You can stop over at El Paso, too, and see a bit of Old Mexico at Juarez, only five minutes distant. Be sure to tour the Apache Trail highway, a one-day side-trip by comfortable motor stage. Through Pullmans on both SUNSET and GOLDEN STATE ROUTES will take you to Globe for the Apache Trail.

Go west one way, return another, by means of Southern Pacific's four routes. See the whole Pacific Coast. No other railroad offers this choice. Stop over anywhere on roundtrip ticket.

Southern Pacific

Four Great Routes

Two very interesting, illustrated books in colors have been prepared for you. They are free. Send your name and address at once to E. W. CLAPP, 310 S. Michigan Blvd., Chicago, for "*Southern Arizona*" and "*How Best to See the Pacific Coast*".

Figure 3.2

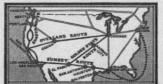

Figure 3.3

the Indian-detour

A motor-link unique in transcontinental rail travel

Beyond the train horizons of New Mexico are hidden primitive Indian pueblos, Spanish missions, prehistoric cliff dwellings and buried cities—all set in the matchless scenery and climate of the Southern Rockies.

Through the Indian-detour—an exceptional motor outing of either two or three days on the Santa Fe way to or from California—one may now explore the Spanish-Indian country with complete comfort. Though temporarily carried far from the railroad, Indian-detour patrons still are guests of the Santa Fe and the Harvey Company. Trained couriers—hostesses, as well as guides—accompany all cars.

Two-day Puyé Detour, $40.00

Three-day Taos-Puyé Detour, $57.50

Rates include every expense en route—motor transportation, courier service, meals and hotel accommodations with bath.

Mr. W. J. Black, Pass. Traf. Mgr.,
Santa Fe System Lines,
904-A Railway Exchange, Chicago, Ill.
   Am interested in "Indian-detour" en route to or from California and Harveycar Motor Cruises Off the Beaten Path.
   Please send me folders and detailed information.

_____

_____

Figure 3.4

"The Blanket"—Taos-Puye Indian-detour, New Mexico—by E. I. Couse, N. A.

Why not, this summer?
gratify that great urge of the wanderlust?
Go - see Far West scenic regions.

Take the Indian-detour in the cool New Mexico Rockies— meet real Indians in their pueblos and see prehistoric cliff dwellings.

—with a Courier-hostess in the party who likes to answer questions.

—And see the dude ranches, mile-deep canyons, sky-high peaks, national parks and national forests.

—with Grand Canyon and Yosemite as crowning glories.

—and at journey's end CALIFORNIA—the land where travel dreams come true.

Santa Fe Summer
daily Xcursions
to California, to the Colorado, Arizona, New Mexico Rockies, and the National Parks.
Santa Fe - cool summer way

mail coupon

Figure 3.5

"the Indian-detour" on their way to California. The visuals show Indians dressed in native costume either dancing what appear to be traditional dances or examining woven blankets. In both instances the people are removed from any historical or physical context. No hint is given that the dances may be staged ones for tourists or that the blankets may be woven in hopes of selling them to those passing through the reservation. There is no indication of anything other than timelessness of the represented culture, certainly no hint of a defeated and demoralized people relegated to government reservations. The detour offers the opportunity to "meet real Indians in their pueblos and see prehistoric cliff dwellings"—all this with an accompanying hostess "who likes to answer questions."

The Burlington Route advertises its Black Hills Detour as an opportunity to realize a fantasy (Figure 3.6). A lone cowboy racing away from a band of marauding Indians turns in order to fire at them. The accompanying text mentions Custer, Wild Bill Hickok, Deadwood Dick, and Calamity Jane and encourages the traveler to relive the days of the Old West again. Burlington promises that "the glamour of adventurous days still lingers."

The Canadian National Railway System urges travel to Alaska—"land of gorgeous scenery where the romance of Gold Rush days still lives" (Figure 3.7). From a promontory, the reader looks down upon a majestic Canadian National steamship sailing through the Inside Passage to Alaska. A collection of white pioneers and Native Americans, who in life were seldom found in close association, are assembled beside an enormous totem pole like actors in the wings waiting to go on stage. This advertisement employs the familiar vantage of many travel advertisements, that of the native looking at the ship in wonder, admiration, and envy. It sets out a social structure that separates those who travel from those who are merely onlookers at their experiences. The prospective tourist is encouraged to send for a booklet on Alaska, the cover of which is illustrated with a native woman carrying her papoose on her back. Time is frozen in this advertisement. Representatives of Alaska's past relive a revised and romanticized version of its history.

These advertisements construct images of Native Americans for the readers of the *National Geographic*: savage attackers of the white settlers, exotic dancers, weavers of quaint blankets, carvers of totem poles, and men whose women carry their babies as papooses. Additionally, these people are subdued but not deracinated. Although their recent cultures may have been fierce and unfriendly, their ancient civilizations are mysterious and worthy of attention. These advertisements depict a characterization of Native Americans as well as the quality of their relationship to pioneers, settlers, and contemporary Americans.

This relationship between Americans of native and immigrant origins is also represented in at least two other advertisements in the 1929 *National Geographic*. A comparison is made between the pioneering efforts of the Packard automobile company and settlers of the American West (Figure 3.8). In the illustration, an Indian guide stands beside a much taller white pioneer who peers into the distance. The Indian scout, with outstretched arm, points out directions to the pioneer.

The most invidious and explicit comparison of Anglo and Native Americans occurs in another Santa Fe advertisement (Figure 3.9). Three smiling white children peer out of a train window above the caption, "Gee! We are going to see real, live Indians." This posture encapsulates the relation between the two cultures in 1929. Indians are oddities to be seen; their lives are different; some real ones still live in the West. Such images as these help maintain the romantic fantasies.

South Africa

The image of South Africa presented in the advertisements of the 1929 *National Geographic* could with very little effort be imagined as contemporary advertisements, especially if airplanes were substituted for ships as the means of transportation. South Africa is mentioned explicitly in only five advertisements, three of which are for Canadian Pacific around-the-world or Southern Hemisphere cruises. They tout South Africa as a land of primi-

Black Hills Detour

on your way to Yellowstone or Glacier Park

Custer . . Wild Bill Hickok . . Deadwood Dick . . . Calamity Jane . . . Here they wrote their glowing passages into the history of the Old West.

Here phantom stage coaches lurch and rumble down the old gold trail from Deadwood Gulch. The ghostly Winchesters echo. And the glamour of adventurous days still lingers.

This summer—live those days again in fancy, the roaring time when hearts were big and trigger fingers whimsical —and a man was never asked his name "back in the states."

Only the Burlington can take you to the Black Hills on your way to or from Magic Yellowstone, Glacier Park or the Pacific Northwest. De luxe, observation-top motors await you. Without delay you start on your unforgettable 200-mile Black Hills tour. Mt. Coolidge, Mt. Roosevelt, State Game Lodge (the "Summer White House") Sylvan Lake, the Homestake Gold Mine.

The entire cost, including motor transportation, meals and hotel accommodations, is only $29.50! Mail the coupon now for the free book which gives you all the details of the Black Hills Detour.

Burlington Escorted Tours — a new, carefree plan of directed travel. Definite cost covering all necessary expenses. Everything planned and paid in advance. Travel expert with each party. Mark coupon for Tours Book.

BARGAIN VACATION FARES—DE LUXE TRAINS

Burlington Route

Burlington Travel Bureau, Dept. NG-5
547 West Jackson Blvd., Chicago, Ill.
Send me your free illustrated book on the Black Hills Detour.

Name ....

Address ....

....

☐ Mark an X here if you wish the Escorted Tour book.

Figure 3.6

Alaska

Land of Gorgeous Scenery Where the Romance of Gold Rush Days Still Lives

Come north this summer. Cruise a thousand miles through the calm waters of the "Inside Passage" to Alaska—land of sky-piercing mountains, giant glaciers, valleys ablaze with wild-flowers—land of romance and gold. A delightful ten-day voyage; stops ashore at Ketchikan, Wrangell, Juneau and Skagway, with their quaint native homes and grotesque totem poles.

From Skagway follow the "trail of '98" through the once dreaded White Pass, across Dead Horse Gulch to Lake Bennet and Whitehorse; on to Dawson and Nome if time permits. See the "ghost towns" which stand as silent and deserted reminders of the Klondike gold rush.

Make this glorious tour to Alaska over the Jasper Park-Pacific Route across Canada—stopover at Minaki in the Canadian Lake and woods Country and at Jasper National Park in the heart of the Canadian Rockies.

The whole trip is one of comfort and relaxation—de luxe train service across the continent—palatial Canadian National Steamers with large airy lounges and smoke rooms—dancing and music—excellent cuisine, deck sports, promenades. Put Alaska on your program this summer

For information on Alaska tours — consult the nearest Canadian National office.

OFFICES

BOSTON 333 Washington St.	**NEW YORK** 505 Fifth Ave.
BUFFALO Liberty Bank Bldg. 420 Main St.	**PHILADELPHIA** Burlington Arcade 1420-22 Chestnut St.
CHICAGO 108 W. Adams St.	**PITTSBURGH** 505 Park Building 355 Fifth Ave.
CINCINNATI Dixie Terminal Bldg. 49 E. Fourth St.	**PORTLAND, ME.** Grand Trunk Ry. Sta.
CLEVELAND 925 Euclid Ave.	**PORTLAND, ORE.** Pacific Building 302 Yamhill St.
DETROIT 1259 Griswold St.	**ST. LOUIS** 314 No. Broadway
DULUTH 420 W. Superior St.	**ST. PAUL** 83 East Fifth Street
KANSAS CITY 705 Walnut St	**SAN FRANCISCO** 689 Market St.
LOS ANGELES 607 So. Grand Ave.	**SEATTLE** 1329 Fourth Avenue
MINNEAPOLIS 518 Second Ave. So.	**WASHINGTON, D. C.** 901—15th St., N. W.

Send for this booklet on Alaska

CANADIAN NATIONAL
The Largest Railway System in America

OPERATING RAILWAYS · STEAMSHIPS · HOTELS · TELEGRAPH AND EXPRESS SERVICE · RADIO STATIONS

Figure 3.7

PACKARD

Packard has pioneered as boldly in modern industry as earlier Americans in opening a western empire to progress

Packard has ever looked beyond the boundaries of accepted practice to new horizons. A policy of pioneering research, established thirty years ago, has guided not only designing engineers, but those charged with the development of Packard manufacturing methods.

Packard technicians have provided the specialized tools and machines, the new steels and the advanced processes for fabricating materials, which translate the original creative engineering into practical usefulness.

Packard engineers have refined and improved the famous straight-eight motor, with its nine-bearing crankshaft. They have perfected the new and unique Packard Shock Absorbing System. And Packard designers have enriched the fundamental beauty and distinction of Packard bodies.

The latest refinements and improvements which have added to Packard's supremacy in the fine car field are the natural result of a spirit never satisfied and an intent ever to excel.

ASK THE MAN WHO OWNS ONE

Figure 3.8

Gee! We are going to see real, live Indians »

Here is a real Out West Outing - the Indian - detour, Grand Canyon, Colorado Rockies, California.

SANTA FE daily FAR WEST Xcursions—this summer—offer you a vacation at very reasonable cost—either individually or by escorted all-expense tours—After California—Hawaii.

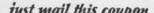

just mail this coupon

W. J. Black, Pass. Traf. Mgr., Santa Fe System Lines, 952 Railway Exchange, Chicago, Ill.
Please mail picture-folders checked below:

☐ California Picture Book ☐ The Indian-detour ☐ Colorado Summer
☐ Grand Canyon Outings ☐ Harveycar Motor Cruises ☐ Escorted all-expense Tours

Santa Fe

Figure 3.9

tive blacks, teeming wildlife, and productive diamond mines. The graphic illustrations in these advertisements show scarified faces, witch doctors, and dancers wearing only loincloths but carrying shields and spears (see Figure 3.10).

The only difference between these advertisements and the South Africa Travel Bureau's official presentation of the country (Figure 3.11) is the latter's even more detailed descriptions:

> South Africa is one of the most modern and progressive sections of the world ... luxurious hotels and railroads, delightful golf and yachting clubs, superb motor roads, and all the comforts and conveniences of modern civilization. But there is also the immensely picturesque native side of South Africa, so alluring to the tourist ... the quaint kraal life ... wild war dances ... weird age-old tribal customs ... the dignified Zulu chief and his retinue of dusky wives ... stalwart warriors with their spears, shields, and knobkerries ... the primitive musical instruments ... the women's fantastic headdresses ... the superstitious mummery of the witch doctor.

Such description sets up a series of contrasts between civilized and primitive people, progress and tradition—and, ultimately, between whites and blacks. The similarity of white South Africa is contrasted for *National Geographic* readers to the "native side of South Africa."

In addition to these advertisements promoting travel to South Africa, the "African jungle" is a prop in an advertisement for Swan fountain pens (Figure 3.12). The copy reads "In the African jungle, in the Australian bush, the effortless glide of a Swan Eternal Pen has written letters home from many a lonely adventurer. On the page of an explorer's diary, an officer's notebook, its velvet touch has helped write the history of an Empire."

The accompanying illustration shows a mustachioed Englishman wearing his pith helmet and bush clothes, with a watch on his wrist and boots on his feet, seated at a small folding table in some nonspecified but identifiably remote corner of the British Empire in Africa. Behind him and facing the bush stands a black man who wears a single piece of cloth wrapped around his body. The Englishman holds a pen and appears to be writing. By contrast, the African holds a raised spear. The relative power of the two men is underscored by the contrast between the pen and the sword.

Thus, the advertisements portraying South Africa operate similarly to the ones dealing with Native Americans. These advertisements depict both an image of otherness as well as a message about the relationship between the indigenous people of South Africa and Westerners. This relationship is never depicted as egalitarian but as one of inequality and dominance. Within the secondary discourses in these advertisements is a characterization of the difference between the lives of other peoples and the lives of the intended audience for these advertisements as well as statements about who is more civilized, more progressive, and more dominant in the affairs of the world.

Relationships of Westerners and Non-Westerners

Advertisements that depict tourists interacting with native peoples clearly show the nonegalitarian nature of their relationship. For example, the United Fruit Company's advertisement (Figure 3.13) for Caribbean travel via the Great White Fleet asks, "Are you *only* an armchair Nomad?" It encourages readers to see the romantic Caribbean for themselves instead of merely imagining what it must be like. This advertisement promises excitement closer to home and without the necessity of a "long, expensive cruise."

Many travel advertisements explain what ocean travel will be like, whether to distant or close ports. This message is simple: The luxury of modern cruise ships as well as on-shore hotels will allow the American visitor the opportunity to visit exotic settings but to live in comfortable surroundings. For example, the Japanese Tourist Bureau (Figure 3.14) invites visitors with the promise that "the ancient and the modern world form one harmonious whole," that they will have "every up-to-date comfort and food to suit [their] taste" yet can "spend

Another Cruise
Around the World

on the
"SAMARIA"
January 26 to June 3, 1924

JAPAN! What a delightful picture of charming landscape, flower festivals of pink and white, fanciful temples and shrines, and amazingly interesting people. Yet Japan is only one of the many fascinating and engrossing countries you will come to know on our 1924 Grand Cruise Around the World.

Sailing Eastward in the Path of Spring, the superb itinerary embraces the ever fascinating Mediterranean and Egypt—India, Dutch East Indies and Straits Settlements, Philippines, South and North China, Cherry Blossom Time in Japan, then homeward via Hawaii, San Francisco, and Panama Canal. 129 joyous days.

The new oil-burning SAMARIA, the ship which proved herself so popular during our 1923 Golden Jubilee Cruise, has again been chartered by us. The renowned Cunard Service—courteous, competent officers—well trained stewards—unexcelled cuisine—will again enhance the pleasure of the voyage.

*Cruise Limited to
400 Guests*

Last but not least, it is a Cook's Cruise, managed by COOK'S TRAVEL SERVICE—the World's Foremost Travel Organization—with its unique and complete chain of permanent offices along the route.

THOS. COOK & SON
245 Broadway   NEW YORK   561 Fifth Ave.
Boston   Philadelphia   Chicago   San Francisco   Los Angeles   Montreal   Toronto   Vancouver

Figure 3.10

Figure 3.11

The SWAN Pen
Pen of the British Empire
SINCE 1843

IN the African jungle, in the Australian bush, the effortless glide of a *Swan* ETERNAL PEN has written letters home from many a lonely adventurer.

On the page of an explorer's diary, an officer's notebook, its velvet touch has helped write the history of an Empire. At the Equator and close to the Pole, the *Swan* ETERNAL PEN has proved its enduring perfection.

Only craftsmanship as fine as that which fashions jewels can achieve such exquisite precision of adjustment, such unfailing continuity of performance. Only a pen made by hand, with the most meticulous care, can be guaranteed, not merely for a lifetime, but eternally.

FROM FIVE TO TEN DOLLARS.

NEW YORK
243 West 17th Street
CHICAGO
209 South State Street

Swan PENS

MABIE, TODD & COMPANY

LONDON ~ PARIS
BRUSSELS ~ BARCELONA
SYDNEY ~ CAPETOWN

Figure 3.12

GREAT WHITE FLEET

Are you *only* an armchair Nomad?

WHISKED AWAY to far-off lands by the magic of the printed page, do you cease to dream of roaming when you close the book? Or do you resolve to see for yourself the romantic Caribbean lands?

A long, expensive cruise is unnecessary. Just a few days south of us lies Cuba, where Havana and Santiago invite you. In Jamaica, Kingston and Port Antonio; in the Panama Canal Zone, Cristobal and Panama City. In Costa Rica is lazy old Port Limon. Santa Marta, Puerto Colombia, and Cartagena will make you want to tarry in Colombia; Guatemala will show you the charm of Puerto Barrios and Guatemala City. In British Honduras you will see brisk little Belize, and in Spanish Honduras, Puerto Castilla and Tela.

Great White Fleet liners leave New York twice weekly and New Orleans three times weekly. Cruises from 9 to 24 days. First class passengers only. All shore trips, hotel and railway accommodations included. Write for complete information to

Passenger Traffic Department
UNITED FRUIT COMPANY
Steamship Service
Room 1624, 17 Battery Place, New York City

CARIBBEAN
~via~
GREAT WHITE FLEET

Make Your New Year's Resolutions in JAPAN

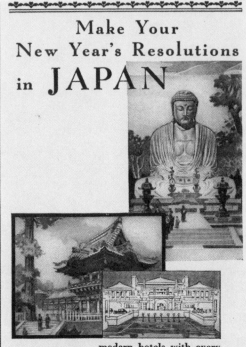

modern hotels with every up-to-date comfort and food to suit your taste.

LET temple bells ring in your New Year spent at the Japanese festival of floats and flowers, the many-colored rites of five days of gaiety,— a thrilling prelude to your winter season in the Island Empire.

Fast modern trains unroll a vista of snow-girt mountains and glittering valleys, and carry you to the skiing and skating in the northern resorts. The fragrant cycle of blossoms beginning in February with the plum, takes deeper color from native pilgrimages. Here the ancient and the modern world form one harmonious whole. You enjoy the comfort of American hotels, and spend delightful evenings in bamboo tea-houses garlanded in wistaria. Ancient shrines and sequestered villages recreate the romance of the past; or you may play golf and tennis. A holiday in fascinating scenes of never-ending beauty!

All details of your trip, including a carefully planned itinerary of Japan's interest points, arranged without charge. Write today for fascinating booklet on Japan.

Steamship Lines operating between the United States and Japan: *Nippon Yusen Kaisha, Osaka Shosen Kaisha, American Mail, Canadian Pacific, Dollar Line.*

JAPAN TOURIST BUREAU

c/o JAPANESE GOVERNMENT RAILWAYS
1 Madison Ave., New York City
and c/o NIPPON YUSEN KAISHA
545 Fifth Ave., New York City

or offices of American Express Co. and Thos. Cook and Sons,
or any tourist or steamship agent

delightful evenings in bamboo tea-houses garlanded in wistaria." In this land "ancient shrines and sequestered villages recreate the romance of the past; or you may play golf and tennis."

Another theme in the travel advertisements is that the visitors can look at but do not have to mingle with, touch, or become involved with the natives. Rather, they can surround themselves with the amenities and comforts of home and venture out into the exotic only in controlled circumstances. Such experiences are a long way from how Boorstin characterizes travel prior to the nineteenth century. These protected interactions with native peoples, cultures, and places are the essence of modern tourism. For example, a Cunard-Anchor West Indies Cruise advertisement (Figure 3.15) offering all the delights of summer during the winter depicts a native boy tending pigs. Presumably both the boy and the pigs will be well out of arm's reach and nose's range, but they will provide backdrops of local color. More explicit depictions show Westerners standing at some distance and looking—or, perhaps more correctly, gawking—at the natives who, unlike the well-turned-out tourists, wear colorful costumes.

Sometimes the relationship is described in the copy, as, for example, in the advertisement in Figure 3.16 and other similar ones in the 1929 *National Geographic:* "Watch the monkeys skipping over the walls of Jaipur … and a stately Indian squat down in the street to make tea on his portable brazier"; "The world is yours. … Native hawkers sell India's treasures for a song … chrysoprase and curios, silks and saris"; "Buy brass bowls by the pound"; "Bring back the world—in your trunk, your picture album, and your heart." The world presented in this manner becomes a curio shop where the astute tourist can collect mementos and gifts at bargain prices. In other words, the world, its peoples, and their artifacts are objects that are there to be possessed either literally or in photographs.

Egalitarian relationships between visitors and the visited were not depicted in any non-Western settings. Hawaii (Figure 3.17) is "the world's enchanted island playground." The Hawaii Tourist Bureau's advertisements show Oriental women

Figure 3.15

CHANGE YOUR MIND

GIVE IT
NEW BEAUTY
NEW INTERESTS
AND NEW EXPERIENCES

CAST off your Occidental worries for a while. Make a cruise Around the World. Feel the spell of the Orient... the languor of starry, scented nights... the mystery of ancient lands. Watch the monkeys skipping over the walls of Jaipur... and a stately Indian squat down in the street to make tea on his portable brazier. Enjoy the musical comedy customs of Korea... where a man shows his top-knot thru a stove pipe hat of wire netting. 33 countries to see... including Indo China and Borneo ... 140 days to absorb them. The luxurious

RESOLUTE   QUEEN OF CRUISING STEAMERS

to connect them. She is experienced, you know ... for this is her 7th Around the World Cruise. So sail eastward from New York January 6th ... on

The Voyage of Your Dreams
arriving in every country at the ideal season.

Rates $2000 and up include an extraordinary program of shore excursions. Write for literature

HAMBURG-AMERICAN
LINE
39 Broadway   New York

Branches in Boston — Chicago — Philadelphia
St. Louis — San Francisco — Los Angeles — Montreal
Winnipeg — Edmonton — Or Local Tourist Agents

standing apart from seated, reclining, and relaxed American tourists. The tourists wear bathing suits and other leisure clothes, whereas the Oriental women are dressed in formal kimonos. Are these geishalike hostesses who only wait to serve? In another advertisement for Hawaii (Figure 3.18), seated tourists in evening dress look upon a native woman dancing the hula in a grass skirt. She is barefoot and scantily dressed; the spectators wear more formal attire. In addition to the differences in clothing, the separation of the visitors from the visited is repeated in a variety of ways throughout the advertisement. Yet another advertisement in the same series (Figure 3.19) both shows and describes the delights awaiting the tourist in Hawaii: "Diving boys plunge from the rail of your ship ... Lei girls greet you with flowers. ... The torches of native fishermen will sparkle to you from a distant coral reef as you sit chatting with old chance-met acquaintances of the Riviera."

Perhaps the most obvious demonstration of the relationship between the visitor and visited is the illustration that appears in a Canadian Pacific ad for a world cruise (Figure 3.20). It is not clear what exact location the picture is intended to represent, but the social structure between the tourist and the native is unmistakable. From the deck of the ship, tourists toss handfuls of coins into the water as natives dive from their canoes for the money. This theme is to be found in any number of advertisements from the 1920s and 1930s (recall Figure 2.8) and illustrates the economic differential between the affluent who can travel and these men who are willing to dive for pennies cast into the sea. What the tourist appears to be doing in search of novel pleasure is quite likely motivated by economic need on the part of the divers.

Images of the West

Advertisements appearing in the 1929 *National Geographic* promote travel to Europe as well as to non-Western countries. The differences between the treatment of these destinations, however, is instructive in understanding the degree to which the

See HAWAII *When the glowing flame trees bloom!*

IN MAY the trees that shade Hawaii's gardens burst into round domes of gold and pink and scarlet flame. You should see these almost-tropic islands of Oahu, Kauai, Maui and Hawaii then—and all through the summer!

Close your eyes, and the cool breeze tells you that you're summering on a northern lake. Open them—and here miraculously are the iridescent sea, the mist-shrouded volcanic peaks, the sunny beaches, coral reefs, and the gorgeous colors of the tropics!

Every day there is golf, on one of a dozen verdant courses. Surfboarding and outrigger-canoeing on Waikiki's cool combers; game-fishing, tennis,

lawn-bowls, motoring, shopping in quaint Oriental bazaars; inter-island cruises and sightseeing among the volcanic wonderlands of Hawaii U. S. National Park.

Hawaii is only 2,000 miles (four to six days' delightful voyage) from the Pacific Coast, and all-inclusive tours range upward from $300 for three weeks, to $400 and $500, including steamers, hotels and sightseeing, for a month's trip. Accommodations, also, equal to those of Europe's most renowned resorts.

Any travel agent can book you direct, via Los Angeles, San Francisco, Seattle or Vancouver. No passport formalities—Hawaii is a U. S. Territory.

HAWAII
The **WORLD'S** *Enchanted Island Playground*

MATSON LINE from SAN FRANCISCO

Sailings every Wednesday and every other Saturday over smooth seas on fast de luxe liners; also popular one-class steamers. Novel entertainment features—glorious fun. Attractive all-expense Island tours. Regular sailings from Seattle and Portland, Ore. See your travel agency or Matson Line: 215 Market St., San Francisco; 535 Fifth Ave., New York; 140 So. Dearborn St., Chicago; 1805 Elm St., Dallas; 723 Seventh St., Los Angeles; 1319 Fourth Ave., Seattle; 271 Pine St., Portland, Ore.

LASSCO LINE from LOS ANGELES

Sailings every Saturday over the delightful Southern route on Lassco luxury liners and popular cabin cruisers. De luxe accommodations; also economy tours on all-expense tickets. Ask at any authorized travel agency or at Los Angeles Steamship Company offices: 730 So. Broadway, Los Angeles; 505 Fifth Ave., New York; 140 So. Dearborn, Chicago; 609 Thomas Bldg., Dallas; 685 Market St., San Francisco; 119 W. Ocean Ave., Long Beach, Calif.; 217 E. Broadway, San Diego, Calif.

HAWAII TOURIST BUREAU

P. O. BOX 3615, SAN FRANCISCO—P. O. BOX 375, LOS ANGELES—P. O. BOX 2120, HONOLULU, HAWAII.

Please send me Hawaii booklet in colors and a copy of "Tourfax" travel guide.   56

Name _____ Street & No. _____ City _____

PRESS OF JUDD & DETWEILER, INC.
WASHINGTON, D. C.

Figure 3.17

"Our movies of Mexico cost us less than the tips."

KEEP YOUR VACATION SCENES and memories fresh at a cost you'll hardly notice . . .

Make movies with Ciné-Kodak Eight, Eastman's new-principle movie camera. Costs only $34.50, and gives you *finished* movies, ready to show on the screen, for less than 10¢ a "shot." The Eight is sturdy, beautifully made—in every way a full-fledged movie camera. Using it is as easy as taking snapshots. See it at your dealer's —he'll show you sample movies, too.

Take the Eight along on your trip . . . you'll bring back so much more. Eastman Kodak Company, Rochester, New York. *If it isn't an Eastman, it isn't a Kodak.*

Makes movies for 10¢ a "shot"

In the movie studios of Hollywood, a shot is one continuous scene of a picture story. The Eight makes 20 to 30 such scenes—each as long as those in the average news reel—on a roll of film costing $2.25, finished, ready to show.

Ciné-Kodak EIGHT

Figure 3.18

DIVING BOYS PLUNGE from the rail of your ship . . . Lei girls greet you with flowers . . .

As you step ashore, you feel that you are the discoverer of a new world where it is never winter or summer, but always June! There are new fragrances of ginger-flowers, *lehua*, plumeria. New jewel colors in the water that caresses the coral sands. A new sense of remoteness from the busy world—yet lacking nothing of the world's accustomed comforts.

Tonight the lilting cadence of a low-voiced Hawaiian song may drift across the hibiscus hedge to the *lanai* of your smart hotel, on a breeze that is just as soft in winter as in summer. The torches of native fishermen will sparkle to you from a distant coral reef as you sit chatting with old chance-met acquaintances of the Riviera.

How *different* it all is—and yet you found Hawaii in less time than it takes to cross the Atlantic.

Golf courses everywhere—along the sea, up in rainbow-festooned valleys, even one where the steam from awesome Kilauea volcano drifts across the greens. Every day you go swimming, surfboarding or out-rigger-canoeing; motor to colorful beaches, stupendous canyons, jungles of giant tree-ferns, and volcanic wonderlands. You enjoy Hawaii's unequalled deepsea game fishing; the native *luaus* and ancient *hulas*; the Oriental bazaars with their countless treasures; the little inter-island cruises.

And best of all, perhaps, the long days and evenings of dreamy, delicious laziness among all the luxuries of the world-famed hotels.

Stay long enough to see it all! Hawaii is only 2,000 miles (four to six days' delightful voyage) from the Pacific Coast; and all-inclusive tours range upward from $400 or $500 including all steamer fares, hotels and sight-seeing for a month's trip with two or three weeks ashore. De luxe accommodations, also, equal to those of Europe's most renowned resorts.

Hawaii is a U. S. Territory and rail-road and travel agents everywhere can book you direct from home, without passports or customs formalities, via Los Angeles, San Francisco, Seattle or Vancouver, B. C. Ask your local agent or mail the coupon for more information today.

＞ ＞ ＞

HAWAII

The WORLD'S *Enchanted Island Playground*

MATSON LINE FROM *San Francisco*
Sailings every Wednesday and every other Saturday over smooth seas on fast de luxe liners; also popular one-class steamers. Novel entertainment features — glorious fun. Matson All-Expense Tours include transportation, hotels, and sight-seeing. See your travel agency or Matson Line: San Francisco, New York, Chicago, Dallas, Los Angeles, Seattle, Portland, Ore.

LASSCO LINE FROM *Los Angeles*
Sailings every Saturday over the delightful Southern route on Lassco luxury liners and popular cabin cruisers. De luxe accommodations; also economy tours on all-expense tickets. Ask at any authorized travel agency or at Los Angeles Steamship Company offices: Los Angeles, New York City, Chicago, Dallas, San Francisco, Long Beach and San Diego, Calif.

For beautiful illustrated booklet in colors, mail this coupon today to . . . **HAWAII TOURIST BUREAU** P. O. Box 3615, San Francisco; 375, Los Angeles; 2120, Honolulu, T. H.

*Name*_____ *Address*_____ 54

PRESS OF JUDD & DETWEILER, INC.
WASHINGTON, D. C.

Figure 3.19

What a marvel of planning!

ROUND-THE- WORLD CRUISE

After seven years of World Cruises... after another year of investigating, arranging, adjusting...this World Cruise!

Alluring odd corners...Bangkok, Sumatra, Formosa. The Java stay stretched to include the Boroboedoer. Ceylon kept at 4½ days by unanimous vote of all the been-theres. India...the cross-India tour...high-spot of all high-spots. 5½ days allotted to Peking and Great Wall region. A full week in Japan... penetrating to Nara, Kyoto, Nikko.

The cruise is timed to put you in Bethlehem for the most impressive of Christmas Eves...in Cairo for the most glamorous of New Year's Eves. Up-country India...Delhi ...Agra...Fatephur-Sekri in cool January. China is celebrating its New Year when you arrive, and Japan will be bursting into plumblossom. Home for Easter.

The cruise unfolds, in progressive panorama, the five great world-epochs, covering Italy, Greece, Egypt, India, China.

The ship again is the Empress of Australia 21,850 gross tons. Marble bath suites. Commodious single cabins. Roman pool. Parischef'd dining-room. From New York, Dec. 2, for 137 glorious days.

SOUTH AMERICA - AFRICA CRUISE

From New York, January 21, 104 days: Duchess of Atholl, 20,000 gross tons. The strangest contrasts, the most curious corners of the world. As low as $1500.

MEDITERRANEAN CRUISES

From New York, Feb. 3, Empress of Scotland...Feb. 13, Empress of France. Both 73 days. As low as $900.

The alluring details are in booklets. If you have a good travel-agent, ask him. Information also from any Canadian Pacific office. New York, 344 Madison Ave. . . . Chicago, 71 E. Jackson Blvd. . . . Montreal, 201 St. James St., West...and 30 other cities in United States and Canada. Personal Services.

Canadian Pacific

World's Greatest Travel System

portrayal of the non-West is indeed a construction of ideological premises about the non-West and of relations between the West and the rest of the world.

In promoting England as the best vacation destination in Europe, the Great Western and Southern Railways of England describe the popular historic personages whose homes can be visited there: Sir Francis Drake (whose figure and ship compose the illustration), Sir Walter Raleigh, Frobisher, Hawkins, Shakespeare, William Penn, and Elihu Yale. In another advertisement by the same sponsor (Figure 3.21), connections are made to earlier personages in English history:

> Step ashore at Southampton, right into the midst of centuries-old pageantry. A biscuit's-throw away … the great New Forest, with its thousand year old oaks … hunting ground of Rufus Redbeard. Beaulieu Abbey built by the Infamous John, from whom the nobles squeezed the Great Charter. Wareham, burial place of the murdered boy king Richard II. Mysterious Stonehenge, as ancient as the moon.

What is most notable about this description—which also applies to descriptions in the advertisements of the Mediterranean but not of South America, the Far East, India, or Africa—is the sense of history and of recognizable personages to whom the modern American is ultimately linked. Thomas Cook's advertisement for a Mediterranean cruise (Figure 3.22) mentions "lands poignant with memories of Moses, Mohammed, Alexander and Caesar, Hannibal and Napoleon." Again, the copy indicates a sense of greater historical depth in Europe and in the Middle East, both places from which America is descended. There are no such connections to be made with other areas of the world, which are treated as historically and culturally unconnected to America and Western civilization.

When places with written histories, like Japan, are described, reference is made to traditions, locations, and practices but not to individuals—as though their history is not the one of such heroes who populate the history of the West.

Figure 3.21   • 69

This examination of the advertisements in the twelve issues of the *National Geographic* magazine that appeared in 1929 demonstrates the kinds of ideas about other peoples and cultures that are repeated frequently in the discourse of advertising. These images, like stereotypes more generally, are based in reality. However, also like stereotypes, they emphasize disproportionally some features while ignoring others. Such a representational process takes the place of other understandings, such as those that might be found in more sympathetic or empathetic descriptions that attempt a balanced description of other peoples and cultures. In time, they are so prevalent that they seem real.

These sorts of representations in popular culture are the ones most widely available to large numbers of Americans. Such images interact with parallel discourses in other popular cultural media, such as the movies, comics, and even novels. They likely constitute as well the essence of the stories that people tell one another in accounts of their touristic adventures abroad.

Different years of the *National Geographic* or other advertisements would yield results similar to those reported here. There will necessarily be alternations in depictions that result from changes in technologies and intercultural relations. And there will even be differences in the intended audiences of advertisements in part because of changing markets. But the system of contrasts that the discourse of advertising establishes between us and them is maintained. In addition to the other work they do, advertisements define both the self and others.

Bibliographic Notes

Histories of the National Geographic Society and its magazine are widely available. Howard S. Abramson's *National Geographic: Behind America's Lens on the World* (New York: Crown, 1987) is a useful introduction, but it has been widely criticized for its biases as a court history. Gilbert Grosvenor gives the society's own viewpoint in *The National Geographic Society and Its Magazine* (Washington, D.C.: National Geographic Society, 1952). The history commissioned by the National Geographic Society, C.D.B. Bryan's *National Geographic Society: 100 Years of Adventure and Discovery* (New York: Abrams,

1987), is a richly illustrated but largely noncritical summary of the society's activities over its first century. A more critical assessment of the National Geographic Society and the magazine is *Reading National Geographic* by Catherine A. Lutz and Jane L. Collins (Chicago: University of Chicago Press, 1993).

Useful overviews of problems of representation are: Jane P. Tompkins, *West of Everything: The Inner Life of Westerns* (New York: Oxford University Press, 1992) and V. Y. Mudimbe, *The Invention of Africa: Gnosis, Philosophy, and the Order of Knowledge* (Bloomington: Indiana University Press, 1988).

A new journal, *Public Culture,* published since 1988, has set as its goal a refinement of scholarly understanding about issues such as cinema, sport, television and video, restaurants, tourism, advertising, fiction, architecture, and museums. Its editorial board has proposed the term *public culture* for such cultural forms instead of the more common *popular culture.*

The Balch Institute for Ethnic Studies provides an exception to the lack of scholarly concern with representations of others in advertisements. In 1984 it mounted an exhibit and published a catalog on *Ethnic Images in Advertising* (Philadelphia: Balch Institute for Ethnic Studies, 1984).

Readers interested in quantitative studies of advertisements, such as content analysis, may wish to consult William Leiss, Stephen Kline, and Sut Jhally, *Social Communication in Advertising: Persons, Products, and Images of Well-being* (New York: Methuen, 1986).

4

Representations of Others, Part 2

Contemporary Print Advertisements

IN THIS CHAPTER I examine a second period in twentieth-century American advertising: the late 1980s and early 1990s. In addition to an opportunity to study more contemporary advertisements for what they have to say about other peoples and cultures, this examination allows me to explore continuities and changes over the years since the advertisements presented in the last chapter were originally published. I focus once again on the secondary discourse in the advertisements in order to understand the ideology of otherness it contains.

I chose the advertisements in this chapter because they deal in one way or another with other peoples and cultures. They originally appeared in a wide variety of popular magazines and are typical of many others. When considered together rather than individually, they reveal patterns in the representations of others contained in contemporary American advertising.

Americans and Foreigners

I begin with two advertisements that convey some general ideas about Americans and their relationship to foreigners. The first advertisement (Figure 4.1) promotes travel to Texas by comparing it to foreign travel. By claiming that Texas natives are friendly and that communicating with them will be easy, this advertisement reminds its audience about the perils inherent in international travel. "Natives" in other countries are undependable and

may even be outrightly hostile. Domestic travel lacks such hazards. The visitor to Texas is promised excitement, relaxation, and a genuine welcome—objectives all tourists probably seek but ones that can be realized close to home by following the advice offered here.

Although this advertisement claims only to be about Texas, it in fact sums up the current fears of many Americans about foreign travel and foreigners: being unwelcome, not being able to manage in another language, and finding oneself involved in threatening situations. Americans are constantly aware of such perils. Hijacked airplanes and hostage taking are facts of modern life and increase the anxiety associated with foreign travel, whether it is for pleasure or business. By contrast, what is promised here is a simple, friendly welcome to a destination where the visitor can be away from home and enjoy security and peace of mind at the same time.

It is also worth noting what is not promised in this advertisement. The close-up photograph shows only the smiling face of an older man dressed in western clothes. There is no suggestion that the tourist can expect to be excessively pampered or waited on hand and foot. Although the man's smile is Texas-wide, there is no indication that his only concern is meeting visitors' needs. There is nothing in the picture to suggest that he is perhaps doing anything more than taking time out of his daily routine to extend a cordial welcome to visitors.

It is also important to note that the cultural heterogeneity and ethnic conflicts that sometimes

Visit A Country Where The Natives Are Friendly And The Language Barrier Is Easily Overcome.

You can see it from coastline to county line. And from ear to ear. It's that famous smile that says you're always welcome in Texas. Where you can take off and visit all kinds of exciting places. Or just sit back and visit with friendly folks.

Texas
It's Like A Whole Other Country.
1-800-88-88-TEX

Either way, you'll be tickled to be here. So call 1-800-88-88-TEX, ext. NGT8 today for your free Texas Travel Package. And head for the land where every mile is interesting. And every smile is genuine. Texas. Where so much is so close to you.

Figure 4.1

erupt in America are glossed over here. Hispanics, African Americans, and Native Americans who also make up a part of the cultural mosaic of Texas go unmentioned. Diversity and difference are not the bases of selling the state to visitors. The Texas represented here is whitewashed and speaks English; cultural and linguistic diversity are airbrushed away.

The advertisement in Figure 4.2 contains further information about foreigners and Americans' relations to them. The advertisement promotes the international delivery service of UPS. Twelve inset pictures show a dozen foreign destinations where letters and parcels can be delivered quickly. Familiar images and icons of these destinations appear in the pictures, but each is also labeled with the country's name. Physical types of people (blond northern Europeans, darker southern ones, Asians, robust individuals of Anglo-Saxon ancestry) appear in stereotypic settings. The audience can quickly make the links: blond = skiing = Norway; robust = outdoors = Australia; Asian = karate = South Korea; and so on. Each individual represents the special qualities of his or her nation's distinctive character.

The UPS international delivery network interlinks the twelve separate individuals, but only to an American sender or business. There is no hint whatsoever that the man in Italy can exchange letters with the woman in Japan or that the Australian rancher can send his parcel to the English businessman, although this may be possible by routing them through the United States. The UPS network is depicted as an American network that articulates each of these countries with the United States. The relationship is international from an American perspective, but it is not global. America stands at the center of an international shipping system, but the links of the various countries are always back to or through the center.

Examination of the advertisements in Figures 4.1 and 4.2 reveals a good deal about the relations of late twentieth-century America to the rest of the world. Like all advertisements, these purport to be about the goods and services proffered. However, they convey in their secondary discourse an ideol-

ogy about the relations of Americans and foreigners that is repeated elsewhere in other advertisements. Such recurrent patterns establish and continually reinforce ideas about social relationships and intercultural exchanges. They describe international relations and the locus of world power. At the core of this discourse are lessons about dominance and hierarchy, subordination and inequality. In their own time and place, these messages about otherness embedded within contemporary advertising are no less important as a form of public instruction than were biblical teachings depicted in the etched windows of Gothic cathedrals or the paintings on cave walls in other ages.

Many of the differences between representations of the West and the non-West that were depicted in the 1929 advertisements are also found in contemporary representations. The West is frequently presented as having history whereas the non-West is often described as having traditions. Western history is venerated and used to explain America's origins; non-Western traditions are exotic yet interesting. Advertisements that depict Europe often show a different kind of foreigner from those that depict the Caribbean or Asia. These are not absolute differences that occur in every depiction but patterns established through frequent repetition.

Another common theme in contemporary advertisements with precedents in the 1929 advertisements is the depiction of the other as feminine or childlike. Feminist criticism of gender representations in advertising, which has been outspoken and strident, seems to have changed neither the depiction of women in foreign contexts nor the use of the feminine metaphor for otherness. But an important difference exists in the representation of otherness as female when the West and the non-West are signified. This difference is demonstrated in advertisements in Figures 4.3 and 4.4.

The Chanel advertisement (Figure 4.3) is typical of many that portray European women. Here a woman conforming to Western ideals of beauty is dressed in the style of French haute couture and exudes luxury. She holds a large bouquet of roses that precisely match her lipstick and the silk rose on her

Now UPS delivers for fewer francs, yen or drachmas than our competition.

At UPS, we're changing the face of the international delivery business. Because we've expanded our service to all of Western Europe, the Pacific Rim, New Zealand, Australia and Canada.

And that means delivery door to door to every single address in every country we serve, with no surcharges for out-of-the-way places.

We'll see that your UPS Letters, Paks and packages move quickly through customs thanks to our Electronic Customs Pre-Alert system that informs officials that your packages are on their way. Our service also includes computerized tracking that enables us to give you a fast reply to your delivery inquiry. Again, we do all this at no added cost.

But what's truly remarkable is that, because of our efficiency, we can do all these things while charging you less than other international delivery companies. Which is important. After all, a drachma saved is a drachma earned.

We run the tightest ship in the shipping business.

UPS

Figure 4.2

IT WOULDN'T BE CHRISTMAS WITHOUT

CHANEL

FASHION. FRAGRANCE. BEAUTÉ.
AT SELECTED FINE STORES AND CHANEL BOUTIQUES.

Figure 4.3

Figure 4.4

hat. She wears jewelry that can only be imagined to be gold. Here, Europe (and France in particular) is represented as feminine. This picture evokes fashion, fragrance, beauty, finery, physical perfection, elegance. This woman and the culture she represents are esteemed. For female readers, she is to be emulated; for males, she is to be sought.

By contrast, the Asian woman in Figure 4.4 is portrayed as submissive and vulnerable. The model wears a silky, kimonolike outfit. This woman, too, connotes beauty, although her beauty is associated with a different aesthetic. The Asian woman is on no pedestal; the essence of her beauty is easier to obtain. The woman is only a model. She is a passive mannequin, a mechanism for displaying expensive clothing. The model has struck a pose that evokes the stereotype of Asian women as submissive. The downward tilt of her head and the childlike way in which her sleeves hang over her hands communicate this. Although she is depicted outside the context of social relationships, it is easy to imagine that she would not dominate her social world.

Of course, foreigners and foreign situations are not always depicted as female. The point is rather that when the metaphor of the female is used, it stands in contrast to what might have been communicated had the representational form been male. Two advertisements for Asian airlines illustrate the differences in what is communicated in such a choice. In Figure 4.5, Singapore Airlines is represented by a nearly full-page picture of a flight attendant. The brief copy that accompanies refers to the service offered by the airline. By contrast, two men—one Japanese, one American—appear in the Japan Air Lines advertisement (Figure 4.6). Here the issues are professionalism, good management, and excellence. There is no question that these men do not serve. Rather, they represent the passengers who will be served. The advertising copy makes it clear that their standards are high. These advertisements thus communicate what feminine versus masculine representations signify.

There are, then, a number of familiar themes in contemporary advertisements depicting foreigners: the potential threat that the unknown represents, the dominance of America over foreigners,

the differences between the veneration of the West and the non-West, and the use of feminine metaphors to convey submissiveness and subordination. But closer study reveals more. Although there are important differences between these contemporary representations of foreigners and those used earlier in the twentieth century, there are remarkable parallels and persistent similarities as well.

Three Categories of Foreigners

In print advertisements appearing in American magazines in the late 1980s and early 1990s, foreigners appear in three main categories: in travel advertisements, in product endorsements, and in advertisements dealing with international business. I examine each of these categories in turn as well as some more specialized situations in which other people and cultures appear in contemporary advertisements.

Foreigners in Travel Advertisements

The most frequent appearance of foreigners in contemporary advertisements is in travel promotions, in which foreigners are presented in conjunction with the destinations advertised by airlines, hotel chains, travel companies, and even governments. In these contexts the foreigners are indigenous and native to the advertised destinations. They are part of what American tourists are encouraged to experience when they go abroad. Some advertisements depict natives in their local contexts; others show American tourists in the foreign destinations. The secondary discourse in them explains the relation of American tourists to those who are native to the countries to be visited.

Travel to Aruba is promoted in the advertisement in Figure 4.7. The inset photos convey to the reader images of both Aruban natives and American tourists. The distinction is simple: Natives smile, work, and dance—all in service of the tourists' needs; meanwhile, tourists do "touristy" things like sunbathe, swim, and relax. Their relationship is analogically that of work to leisure, of server to served, of production to consumption. Moreover, they

WE FLY THE WORLD'S MOST MODERN FLEET ACROSS FIVE CONTINENTS.

Singapore Airlines now flies to 57 cities in 37 countries with inflight service even other airlines talk about.

SINGAPORE AIRLINES

Singapore Airlines is a partner in the American Airlines AAdvantage® program. AAdvantage® is a registered service mark of American Airlines, Inc. American Airlines reserves the right to change AAdvantage program rules, regulations, travel awards and special offers without notice, and to end the AAdvantage program with six months notice.

Figure 4.5

Why JAL?

"I like organizations that pay attention to details. I feel at home."

Akio Morita
Chairman of the Board &
Chief Executive Officer
Sony Corporation
Tokyo, Japan

"I respect an operation when it's managed by true professionals."

Jeffrey A. Barks
Associate Dean for Master's
and Bachelor's Programs
Sloan School of Management
M.I.T.

In a world of increasingly unpredictable service standards, Japan Air Lines remains a reference of professionalism. That's one of the reasons why more people from all over the world choose JAL to fly to the Orient than any other airline. On your next trip to the Orient, fly the airline that's run the way you'd run an airline. For reservations, call your travel agent or Japan Air Lines directly at 1-800-JAL-FONE.

JAPAN AIR LINES
Comfortably ahead, worldwide.

Tokyo   Osaka   Seoul   Hong Kong   Beijing   Shanghai   Manila   Singapore   Bangkok   and Beyond

Figure 4.6

dress differently and they look different physically. Most Americans in the advertisements are blond and blue eyed; natives are nearly always darker.

The Aruba advertisement contains much more to be decoded. The copy describes the beach as "bride-white" and the sea as turquoise. It promises the leering and wishful reader "whatever makes you happy." The turquoise skirts of the dance troop are lifted; a single dancer in another photo invites with outstretched arms. The Third World as feminine persists in this advertisement; the visual metaphor of sexual availability, receptivity, and submission continues.

Although this relationship of the visitor to the visited is easily available in the advertisement and requires little effort on the part of the reader to understand, some other aspects of the relationship are not as readily apparent. For example, despite the many pictures in the advertisement, not one of them shows any direct interaction between the tourists and the native Arubans. Each set of people interact with one another—tourists swim and sun together, natives dance or work together—but these lines are not crossed. The activities of the natives are also limited. Arubans are not shown in family contexts, in work not associated with tourism, nor in any leisure activities of their own. Rather, they are depicted as happy and ready to please.

Analytic commentaries such as this are sometimes dismissed as idiosyncratic interpretations of particular advertisements. Yet these patterns and other congruent ones recur through so many travel advertisements that it becomes difficult to dismiss them outright. Although particular pieces of such interpretations may be open to question, the repeated nature of these themes makes it difficult to dismiss this reading of their meaning altogether as, for example, in the following advertisements promoting travel to Mexico, the Bahamas, Hawaii, China, and even Europe.

The advertisement for Mexico (Figure 4.8) contains many similarities. Enrique works while the American women admire his painting. He is removed from his own personal and domestic context and depicted in his role as a maker of cultural representations. He simultaneously represents what it is that natives do—that is, smile, serve, and cater to tourists—and quite literally represents in his own painting what it is that they have come to see: His painting has made the sky bluer, the flowers lusher, the colors fuller, and it has removed the blemishes of unsightly electric wires draped on the outside of buildings and signs hung off center. The tourists' delight is palpable.

Moreover, the usual relationship of male domination and female subordination in advertising is momentarily reversed in this advertisement. The tourists are women, but they are Americans; the native is a man, but he is a Mexican. The reversal of the dominance hierarchy, of who works and who does not, of who serves and who is served, is a visual depiction of the understanding that American women are superordinate to foreign men. In the advertisement they talk, they admire, they find pleasure in his work. His work in turn is done to serve their needs. Enrique's motivation for painting is surely economic. His livelihood depends on their pleasure in his work. Also notice that only his first name is given. This puts the unnamed women in the relationship of that of employer to employee, of structural superior to status inferior.

It is also possible to interpret the sexual innuendos in this advertisement, conveyed through its sensual visual and linguistic imagery. In addition, there are other salient issues, such as the allusion to history that is not developed beyond conveying a sense of the presence of tradition and of things old. The ambience includes historical depth, but the specifics of that history are left uncomprehended; issues such as colonial domination and local resistance that constitute it go unexplored.

Similar themes resonate in the advertisement for the Bahamas (Figure 4.9). New Providence Island, Nassau, is represented by a woman whose slopes and curves rise out of blue water. Her beaches are likened to "cream colored silk." Her hotels are "great" and "big." All around her are "sleek white yachts with rich men inside." The tourist is invited to partake of the available sensuality of this nearby but nonetheless exotic foreign destination. It does not take much effort to think of conquest, domina-

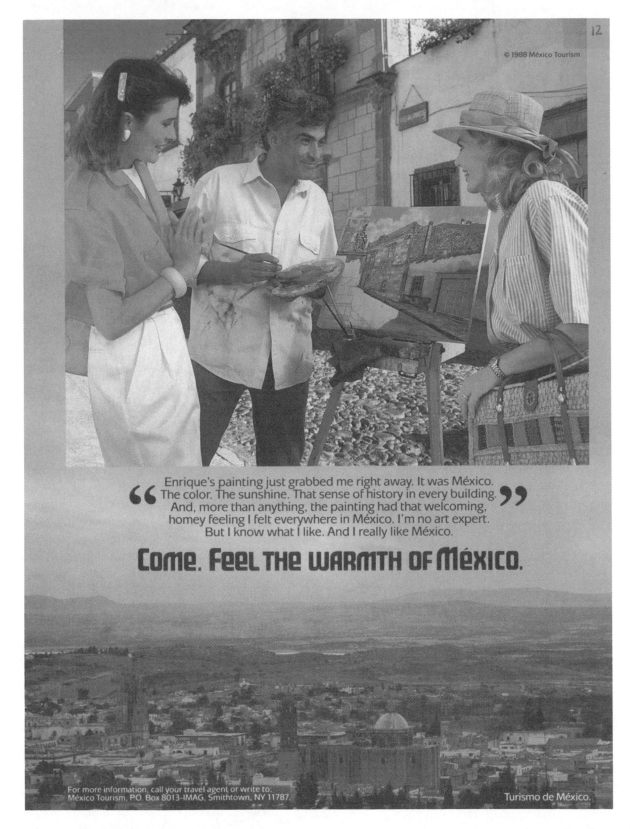

"Enrique's painting just grabbed me right away. It was México.
The color. The sunshine. That sense of history in every building.
And, more than anything, the painting had that welcoming,
homey feeling I felt everywhere in México. I'm no art expert.
But I know what I like. And I really like México."

Come. Feel the warmth of México.

For more information, call your travel agent or write to:
México Tourism, P.O. Box 8013-IMAG, Smithtown, NY 11787.

Turismo de México.

Figure 4.8

I've got the bluest waters in the world.
Beaches like cream colored silk.
Great big romantic hotels.
And all around me, I've got sleek white yachts with rich men inside.
I'm New Providence Island. Nassau.
Just 35 minutes from Miami and that's what I call conveniently located.

Let's assume I'm an Island.

700 Bahama Islands

BAHAMA ISLANDS TOURIST OFFICE. 100 SOUTH BISCAYNE BOULEVARD. MIAMI, FLORIDA

Figure 4.9

tion, subordination, and submission. The Bahamas represent a receptive and willing potential partner in a relationship. The tourist is enticed by the images with which the woman/the destination describes herself. She promises a thrilling seduction. The excitement is heightened by lure and tease. "Let's assume I'm an island," the copy beckons.

The advertisement for the Polynesian Cultural Center in Hawaii (Figure 4.10) reiterates the relationship of the tourist to the native. The advertisement explains that no passport is required to visit 42 acres of authentic South Pacific villages that are recreated and displayed in Hawaii. The Polynesian Cultural Center claims to have been "Hawaii's number one visitor attraction for over twenty-five years." After all, it contains what tourists hope to see: representations of the exotic in a safe, controlled environment. The woman in the picture, posed for a photographic souvenir of her travel experience, is flanked by two men who also face the camera sporting posed smiles. They are dressed in exotic native clothing; their faces are painted with tribal markings; they wear necklaces of carved bone and shell. They represent the foreign, but they are friendly. Their occupational labor is to enhance the enjoyment of the tourist in the act of tourism—in this instance by posing with her in a photograph that will prove to those at home that she has really been to the South Seas. She interacts in this limited way with men who are like servants or employees to her. She has paid the price of admission; their smiles are a part of the entertainment. As in the advertisement promoting Mexican tourism, the tourist and her needs dominate the relationship. The men are of the Third World; they are her subordinates. Here once again the status of the American woman is elevated above that of foreign men in the discourse of advertising.

This advertisement continues the instruction noted in Chapter 3 concerning the composition and subject matter of travel photographs. In the intervening years since the camera first became a part of the tourist's usual equipment, the regularity of subject matter for travel photographs has become sustained. The instruction can be more subtle, just as the camera—out of sight and unmen-

tioned—is understood to be an integral part of the travel experience.

China, the world's most populous nation and one of the most exotic and enigmatic destinations for Western tourists, is the subject of the advertisement in Figure 4.11. A tidbit of history mentions an unnamed emperor. A serene body of water dominates the visual representation and shimmeringly mirrors oddly shaped mountains. The tourist is promised a China that few other visitors uncover and is assured that the Chinese government will accord special status and privileges, including visits to Chinese homes. Although it is not easy to see people in the picture in the advertisement, it is nonetheless easy to infer the relationship that the Chinese will have to the American tourists. The Chinese will be there as part of the scenery; they will even perform their parts when the status of "honored guest" allows the tourist seemingly unique visits into selected homes; the landscape, culture, and history of China will provide the raw materials that will enhance the visitor's travel experiences.

Europe, at least as it is depicted in the advertisement in Figure 4.12, is even more enigmatic. On the one hand, the advertisement evokes European aristocracy. In the minds of many Americans, an English fox hunt stands as the symbol of aristocratic tradition, wealth, and ultimate leisure—a culture that can put American culture to shame. This advertisement depicts a life-style that is more expensive to maintain than one involving occasional vacations to the Caribbean or the South Pacific. And perhaps most important of all, the natives in this advertisement may be even more powerful and dominant than Americans.

On the other hand, by showing the English countryside from the air and with the shadow of an American Airlines jet cast upon it, the advertisement exhibits American technological power and freedom to travel. The English aristocracy are literally in the penumbra of Americans and their know-how. The hunting horse may be an ancient part of British culture, but American technology is superior. One plane dwarfs several horses and their riders. Engine power is compared to horsepower. The

Put on a happy face!

face to face at the Polynesian Cultural Center

At the Polynesian Cultural Center, meet the many happy faces that comprise Polynesia. Taste the exotic flavors of our **Ali'i Luau**. Learn exciting games and dance to the music as you explore 42-acres of authentic South Pacific villages: Samoa, Maori New Zealand, Tahiti, Fiji, Tonga, the Marquesas and old Hawaii.

See why we have been Hawaii's #1 visitor attraction for over 25 years, as we open both our homes and hearts to you and teach you the greeting word of our native homes.

With our lagoon-laced landscape, waterfalls and lush tropical flora, a day at the Center is a warm and memorable experience, a chance to travel to all of Polynesia in a single day.

Have a *face-to-face* encounter with the South Pacific at the Polynesian Cultural Center and celebrate with us centuries of Polynesian culture — no passport required.

POLYNESIAN CULTURAL CENTER

Open Mon-Sat (closed Sunday) from 12:30 pm. For information and reservations, contact your travel agent or tour operator. In Hawaii, call **293-3333** or stop by our Waikiki Ticket Office in the Royal Hawaiian Shopping Center, Bldg. C ground floor. From the mainland, call **tollfree: 1-800-367-7060.**

Figure 4.10

Figure 4.11

No one can show you Europe quite like American can. And this year, American can take you to more of it than ever. With service to thirteen wonderful European cities. Including new service to Lyon, Hamburg, Stockholm, and Brussels.* Plus, we offer affordable Fly AAway Vacations packages to all of them. As well as the opportunity to earn AAdvantage® miles. It's all designed to show you Europe from a point of view that's distinctly American. **American Airlines**
For more information, call American or your Travel Agent. *Something special to Europe.*

AAdvantage® is a registered service mark of American Airlines, Inc. American Airlines reserves the right to change AAdvantage program rules, regulations, travel awards and special offers without notice, and to end the AAdvantage program with six months notice. *Service begins May 1989. Subject to government approval.

Figure 4.12

camera angle allows the viewer to look down upon the English, to conquer them visually, to remove them from their lofty places. Thus the pattern of dominance and subordination that has been found in other travel advertisements also appears in this advertisement promoting European travel. The heading might just as well have read "Foreigners. From an American Point of View."

Product Endorsements

Foreigners appear in product endorsements in two different ways. In some advertisements the foreigner is shown in association with the creation of a product indigenous to his (or, less often, her) country. Juan Valdez, a fabricated character known to many Americans because of his repeated appearance in advertisements for Colombian coffee, is a prototype of this kind of advertising. The setting is typically exotic, romantic, and bucolic; it might even be a touristic destination. But Juan Valdez is not a tourist. Although his work is romanticized, he is always shown at work. The critical feature of these advertisements is the depiction of the foreigner as working.

It is worth remembering that nineteenth-century and very early twentieth-century advertisements in America often displayed the factory or production process. Roland Marchand has suggested that such displays were similar to the replication of industrial production processes that were commonplace in the world's fairs of this same time period. It is his contention that these displays answered the curiosity of Americans about where all the new goods originated. Judith Williamson further argues that a major function of contemporary advertising is to mystify consumption by separating it from production. In this way the goods can be sold at higher prices to those who produce them. The added values contributed by the process of mystification help justify the discrepancy between the price paid for labor and the cost of goods.

Foreigners are also used to endorse products that have little or nothing to do with their country or nationality. For example, Colgate-Palmolive has the Colgate Wisdom Tooth explain the technical details of the promoted brand of toothpaste along with the advantages of using it (Figure 4.13). The character, a wise old Asian man, is fabricated on the idea that in Far Eastern cultures wisdom and age are linked. Although most Americans would not be able to give much detail about the nature of Asian wisdom, many know of Confucius and his sayings. To understand the advertisement, the reader need not know that the model who appears in the photographs is actor Pat Morita. All that is necessary is to know that Asian old men are supposed to be quite knowledgeable. The advertisement draws on this understanding for its meaning, and at the same time, in doing so, it reinforces this belief about Asian culture. The Asian man is only a vehicle for communicating information about Colgate toothpaste, but the toothpaste advertisement is not overtly a vehicle for communicating information about Asia. That it does so—even when it does not seem to—is precisely the point about how the secondary discourse about images of otherness becomes a primary basis for our beliefs about foreigners.

The same principles apply to the advertisement for Christiana lingerie (Figure 4.14), which depicts a black model wearing designer lingerie and riding on the back of a large animal, possibly a camel. The fuzzy outlines of palm trees in the background and the unfamiliar weapon or implement in her hand rounds out the image. Although this woman is perhaps an American, she portrays a foreigner, quite probably an African. Because she is dressed in expensive clothing and riding upon a draped animal, it is easy to imagine that she is a princess in a jungle kingdom. The black model and her accoutrements evoke this line of thought. Yet she is merely a vehicle for demonstrating the elegance of a brand of very expensive lingerie.

This advertisement has nothing to do with Africa. There is no hint that the clothes are made in Africa; in fact, the copy refers only to "fine European lingerie." But this advertisement repeats and reconstructs Western ideas about Africa, its foreignness, and its primitive nature. The reader is encouraged to draw deeply from associations about Africa—such as the imagined raw sexuality of black women—and to link these with the clothes being promoted. In making this unspoken connection,

SHOULD ONE FIGHT TARTAR? OR PLAQUE?

YES. —The Colgate Wisdom Tooth

Like many things in life, your mouth has natural enemies continually causing it trouble. Two of them are tartar and plaque.

Tartar is crusty, and can make your teeth ugly and yellow. Plaque is invisible, sticky, harmful bacteria constantly forming on your teeth.

Luckily, there is Colgate Tartar Control toothpaste. Not only does Colgate fight ugly tartar build-up, brushing with it also helps remove harmful plaque. This is one toothpaste that really works hard to help keep your teeth clean.

No wonder Colgate Tartar Control is the Wise Choice. Considering what tartar and plaque can do to your teeth, would it be wise for you to use anything less?

The Wise Choice.

Figure 4.13

Christiana
L I N G E R I E

Swimwear from LaPERLA

*Fine European lingerie and designer swimwear
combined with exquisite service.*

We have only the best for you.

a Torie Steele boutique

414 North Rodeo Drive, Beverly Hills, California 90210 (213) 271-5150

Figure 4.14

the advertisement restates such less than fully articulated ideas about Africa that are present in Western culture.

There is also reference to the "exquisite service" offered by the boutique sponsoring the advertisement. A careful reading may invite the reader to link the black model, the chains on the animal, *service*, and perhaps other aspects of the advertisement. Thus this is both an advertisement for what it purports to be about and a lesson that instructs the reader about black women and about Africa.

By contrast, the advertised commodity and foreignness are not overtly related to one another in several contemporary fragrance advertisements like the one in Figure 4.15. Xi'a Xi'ang is linked to images of China. The connection of the perfume to the Far East is not made explicit. Is it merely inspiration, or do its ingredients come from there? There is no hint that the perfume is manufactured in China, despite its Chinese name. Similarly, another fragrance, Shalimar, is linked to India. Its advertisements tell readers that it was inspired by the love story associated with the Taj Mahal. In this way the exoticism, romance, and beauty of Asia are transferred directly to the perfume. A third fragrance is called Safari. Exotic visual imagery links it to the mystery and adventure of Africa. The model who always appears in the advertisements is a white adventuress of the bygone age of propeller planes and leather trunks. In all three instances history is appropriated and transformed to serve the purposes of advertising. Other people and their cultures are "Orientalized." These advertisements do not tell about China, India, or Africa from the point of view of the people who live there but of those who romanticize, exploit, and conquer them.

Each of these advertisements conveys information about a foreign part of the world and the people who live in it. The reader can compare what these advertisements say about South America, China, Africa, and India. The messages are not the same, nor do they appear in these advertisements for the first time. Rather, they are part of a repeated discourse that informs our understandings of other places and people as it purports to be conveying information about products that are actually Western

in manufacture. The advertisements borrow from our culture's ideas about others to promote these brands, but they simultaneously regenerate the very ideas about foreigners that they draw upon.

Advertisements for International Business

With the advent of widespread international and global business have come advertisements offering a variety of services to those who engage in such activities. The overt themes of this advertising are convenience and expediency in conducting business abroad and the promise of the comforts of home and/or accommodations and amenities that combine the best from both worlds. Much airline and hotel advertising falls into this category, as, for example, the advertisements for Singapore Airlines and Japan Air in Figures 4.5 and 4.6. These advertisements promise to facilitate international business and to combine homelike comfort with the finest service traditions in Asian culture. The overall import of such advertising is to downplay otherness and to emphasize commonalities between Americans and foreigners. When business is at stake, foreignness is inconvenient and intrusive. By contrast, when tourism is the issue, foreignness is a commodity to be celebrated and sold.

The issue of strict subordination of foreigner to American is a complex one in business advertising. An advertisement for Nikkei (Figure 4.16) demonstrates how indirectly subordination and dominance are addressed in the business context. "When Nikkei talks, Japan listens" plays on the E. F. Hutton television commercials that are already familiar to American audiences ("When E. F. Hutton talks, people listen"). This intertextual reference buttresses Nikkei's message. The legacy of understanding that the mere mention of the E. F. Hutton name is enough to hush a crowd, make heads turn, and cause people to eavesdrop is borrowed and transferred to Nikkei. The message here is that Nikkei is a powerful information broker just as E. F. Hutton plays that role in the United States. But this message has a different audience from that of Hutton advertising: Its intended audience is American businessmen and -women, who are told that Japanese people listen to what Nikkei has to say

Figure 4.15

When Nikkei Talks, Japan Listens.

At times, Japan's economic triumphs seem even more remarkable at home than they do overseas. How it all comes together with such uncanny synchronicity can often suggest something truly miraculous.

Take a closer look though, and you discover some very basic reasons for this well-managed success, the most obvious being the consistently high level of business information.

Which brings us to *Nikkei*.

Nikkei is many things to many people: It's *The Nihon Keizai Shimbun, the world's largest selling business daily,* and specialized papers in each of the areas of marketing, finance and industry. It's advertising with more impact per yen than any source around. Plus television, databases and much more. That's why we say when *Nikkei* talks, Japan listens.

Oh yes, *Nikkei* speaks English, too. With media like *The Japan Economic Journal,* and *Nikkei Telecom® II—Japan Financial News & Data,* the most complete English database on Japanese business available.

So if you're interested in doing business in— or with—Japan, we suggest one very good place to start. The source most business people in Japan count on for ideas, opportunities and inspiration. The source that listens as well as it talks.

Nikkei.

NIKKEI

Nihon Keizai Shimbun, Inc. 1-9-5 Otemachi, Chiyoda-ku, Tokyo 100-66, Japan Tel: (03) 270-0251 Telex: J22308 NIKKEI
Nihon Keizai Shimbun America, Inc. *New York Office:* Suite 1802, 1221 Avenue of the Americas, New York, NY 10020 U.S.A. Tel: (212) 512-3600
Los Angeles Office: 725 South Figueroa Street, Suite 1515, Los Angeles, CA 90017 U.S.A. Tel: (213) 955-7470
Nihon Keizai Shimbun Europe Ltd. *London Office:* Bush House, Aldwych, London WC2, U.K. Tel: (01) 379-4994
Frankfurt Office: Kettenhofweg 22, 6000 Frankfurt/M 1, West Germany Tel: 069-720214

Figure 4.16

about economic matters, and American business-people can have this information in English through Nikkei's English-language services. Thus the advertisement conveys the ideas that knowledge is power, that the Japanese have economic power because they may have superior knowledge, but that Americans can adjust this power imbalance by subscribing to Nikkei. Read in this manner, the advertisement is about competition among businesspeople, about who has more power derived from greater knowledge, and ultimately about dominance and subordination. Moreover, this advertisement offers a key to overcoming the difficulties that differences between countries and customs present.

Some Additional Issues

Before concluding my examination of contemporary representations of foreigners, I turn to two additional and specialized depictions of foreigners that are contained within contemporary advertisements: those that discuss foreigners as threatening American superiority in some way and those dealing with the needs of poor children in foreign contexts. Although less frequent than the three prevalent contexts in which foreigners appear, these depictions also embody parts of the contemporary American ideology about others.

Threats from Abroad

The threat that foreigners pose to American personal and cultural well-being is another theme within the discourse of contemporary advertising. The advertisement in Figure 4.17 blatantly addresses Americans' xenophobia in general and fear of economic dependency on foreigners in particular. The smirking Arab, bearing strong resemblance to the Ayatollah Khomeini, holds the sad, dwarfed Uncle Sam by his little finger. The copy puns strong foreign relations, here seen as negative dependency rather than positive alliances. The advertisement promotes energy independence, which in turn is allied to cultural and political independence. America's relationship with the rest of the world—

as the majority of advertisements depicting foreigners instruct us—is not one of equality but one of ascendancy and superiority. That America should fall to a position beneath a more powerful foreign country is perceived as threatening, a sign of political, economic, and cultural weakness. This advertisement is propaganda in its simplest terms.

Another kind of threat from foreigners is ownership of America by non-Americans. The Japanese in particular are feared in this regard. They produce superior electronic equipment and automobiles that rival the best from other countries in price and performance, and they have begun to purchase American real estate, factories, and businesses. This is a second sort of invasion by the Japanese. The legacy of World War II is not forgotten in the cultural memory of Americans. Many see the rise of the Japanese on the world scene as both wrong and threatening. The advertisement in Figure 4.18 attempts to rectify this imbalance. The Dodge Colt is both an American and a Japanese car. It carries the American name, but it is built in Japan. What better way to have the best of Japan but to contain it within the orb of American patriotism and economic control? By claiming that "Colt" is "all the Japanese you need to know," this advertisement also spells out what is important in the relationship of Americans to the Japanese. The product of Japanese design and manufacturing is what is important about Japan; other things do not matter. The relationship proposed here is one of the familiar theme of dominance. In the new colonialism proposed in the Dodge Colt advertisement, the reader is urged to take from the Japanese what is most useful and not to bother with more complex and probably uncomfortable aspects of a relationship.

The Needy Foreign Child

At least five different international relief organizations regularly appeal to Americans to share their affluence with needy children, most often those in the Third World countries of Latin America, Asia, and Africa (see Figure 4.19). The advertisements attempt to arrest the attention of the reader, to engage them long enough to convey information about the desperate plight of poor children abroad,

IMPORTED OIL STRENGTHENS OUR TIES TO THE MIDDLE EAST.

Last year, almost 40 percent of all the oil we used came from foreign countries. Much of that from the unstable Middle East. And this dependence on foreign oil is growing.

The more we use nuclear energy, instead of imported oil, to generate electricity, the less we have to depend on foreign nations.

The 110 nuclear electric plants in the U.S. have cut our foreign oil dependence by over three billion barrels since the first Arab oil embargo. And they have cut foreign oil payments by over 100 billion dollars.

But 110 nuclear plants will not be enough to meet our growing electricity demand. More plants are needed.

If we are going to keep our energy future in our own hands, we need to rely more on energy sources we can count on, like nuclear energy.

For a free booklet on nuclear energy, write to the U.S. Council for Energy Awareness, P.O. Box 66103, Dept. AY12, Washington, D.C. 20035.

U.S. COUNCIL FOR ENERGY AWARENESS

Nuclear energy means more energy independence.

Figure 4.17

Colt is now a horse of a different 外観.

We're not talking about a decal here and a door handle there.

Colt has been *totally redesigned*. To some incredibly high standards: Yours.

Case in point: the new Colt 3-door, designed and built in Japan. With lots of excellent improvements that go considerably beyond its aerodynamic new profile.

Its impressive list of standard features includes power brakes, rack and pinion steering, styled steel wheels, full carpeting, a handy **$6678*** split fold-down rear seat and a

*Base sticker price at time of publication close. Excludes title, taxes and destination charges. Dealer has details. 3/36 bumper to bumper warranty that covers the entire car for 3 years or 36,000 miles† And

3/36
Bumper To Bumper Warranty
†See limited warranty at dealer, restrictions apply. Excludes normal maintenance, adjustments and wear items.

when you compare it to a lot of other imports, Colt stands out even more. It has almost twice the cargo room of a Nissan Sentra and a spirited 1.5 liter EFI engine that's more powerful than theirs. Even more gratifying, the Colt is hundreds less than a Sentra.**

To see just how far Colt has come, test drive one at your Plymouth or Dodge dealer. And get the value, reliability and features you want. At a price that hasn't gone through the 天井破り.

優秀 Colt
It's all the Japanese you need to know.

Dodge Plymouth
IMPORTS

Figure 4.18

Five things you can do for 72¢ or less...

1

Enjoy a cup of coffee...

2

Pick up a newspaper...

3

Buy a few stamps...

4

Have a soft drink...

5 Or make a lasting difference in the life of a child and family overseas through Foster Parents Plan.

Here at home, 72¢ is the kind of pocket change you spend every day without thinking much about it. But for a child overseas, born into a world of desperate poverty, it can lead to a future full of promise and achievement.

Your spare change can change the life of a child. Forever.

As a Foster Parent, you'll be helping a needy child in the most critical areas of development. Like education. Better nutrition. Improved health. At the same time, your help will give your Foster Child the gift of hope.

It's hope that springs from Foster Parents Plan's comprehensive programs, built on your support combined with the hard work and determination of your

Foster Child's family to help themselves. Programs that produce ways to make a better living. That build confidence and self-sufficiency, and that result in long-lasting improvements for *all their lives.*

What's more, you'll be able to share in these accomplishments through photographs, progress reports and letters about your Foster Child and family.

Don't wait—a child needs your help now.

Think about all the good you can do for just 72¢ a day, the cost of a morning coffee break. Then send your love and support to a child and family overseas, who need a chance for a better life. Please, do it now.

To start helping even faster, call toll free:

1-800-225-1234

Detach and mail or call toll free today.

Send to:
Kenneth H. Phillips, President
Foster Parents Plan, Inc. • 157 Plan Way • Warwick, RI 02886

I want to become a Foster Parent to:

☐ **The child who has been waiting the longest,** or as indicated:

☐ Boy ☐ Girl ☐ Either

☐ Any Age ☐ 6–8 ☐ 9–11 ☐ 12–14

☐ Colombia   ☐ Sri Lanka   ☐ Mali
☐ Guatemala   ☐ Thailand   ☐ Sierra Leone
☐ Kenya   ☐ Ecuador   ☐ Sudan
☐ Philippines   ☐ India   ☐ Zimbabwe

☐ Enclosed is a check for $22 for my first month's sponsorship of my Foster Child. Please send me a photograph, case history, and complete Foster Parent Sponsorship Kit.

☐ I am not yet sure if I want to become a Foster Parent, but I am interested. Please send me information about the child I would be sponsoring.

J405

☐ Mr.   Mrs. ☐
☐ Miss   Ms. ☐

_____

Address _____ Apt. #

City _____ State _____ Zip

Founded in 1937, Foster Parents Plan is the leader in combining family assistance programs, community development, and personal communications between Foster Parent and Foster Child. These comprehensive programs provide long-term solutions to the unique problems facing Foster Children and their families. As a non-profit, non-sectarian and non-political organization, we depend on Foster Parents to make our work possible. A copy of our financial report is available, upon request, from New York Dept. of State, Office of Charities Registration, Albany, N.Y. or Foster Parents Plan. Your sponsorship is tax deductible.

 Foster Parents Plan.
Help so complete, it touches a child for life.

Figure 4.19

and to motivate monetary contributions to assist. On the surface, this is a highly meritorious effort of utter altruism on the parts of the relief agencies and the donors. More deeply, the relationship that such services create is quite similar to those seen in the contexts of tourism and business.

Although the appeals vary somewhat, certain recurrent patterns characterize this advertising. The children appear in black-and-white close-ups that bring the audience into an uncomfortable degree of intimacy with the children and their problems. The children stare into the camera; they do not smile; their faces are often dirty. Shot from an adult's eye level, the pictures show the children looking up to the reader, on whom they are completely dependent. The copy conveys the message that the reader holds the ability to modify the children's circumstances and is thus responsible to some extent for their plight. This is compelling advertising; it communicates its message forcefully.

What kind of relationship with the needy children is offered to the able reader? Through the reader's money, the children can live better and healthier lives. if lucky, they might even become educated. For a regular sustaining donation, the reader is offered a continuing relationship with the child. Letters thanking the donor will be forthcoming. The children will become beneficiaries of the largess of affluent Americans who by putting aside a relatively small amount of money can make a big difference in the lives of others. For the price of a cup of coffee, a relationship can be established that can transform the life of one of the world's poorest people.

In one sense it is heartless to criticize efforts such as these. It would be a serious misreading of this analysis to understand the comments that follow as disapproving of the motives and efforts being made. Rather, I attempt to place such activities in a broader context and to relate them to other types of relationships between Americans and foreigners. Perhaps a good beginning would be to attend to what is never mentioned in this advertising: The needy children are depicted without social relationships of any sort. As far as the reader can tell, they have no parents, no siblings, no families at all.

There is no indication that their governments provide any sort of assistance. The children stand alone. Only the rich American looms on a distant horizon as a possibility for placing these lonesome children in stable relationships.

Also not addressed in this advertising are the fundamental causes of the problems of world poverty in the first place. For example, low prices paid to coffee producers on the world market might be understood as an economic cause of the poverty. Peasant parents work for low wages on their own or other's farms, and their children may even assist in the farm labor. When the American who sets aside the money for a cup of coffee and sends it to a relief organization initiates assistance to the world's poor, such an effort—although laudatory—is a mere drop in the bucket. Better working conditions for adults and children, higher wages for labor, and improved prices to producers might have sustained impact on the situations that are described. But this would challenge the larger system of relations that ties the world together in an economically interdependent network. If coffee cost more, then the American might have less to give to such causes. Similarly, the problems to be addressed might be fewer. Such a radical alteration in relationships of dependency would change the balance of power. Domination and subordination would each be lessened. The individual donor might disappear and social services might be managed governmentally. This would transform the very nature of individualism, of private incentives, and of philanthropy. It would alter relations between the dominant and the subordinate.

In addition to this line of criticism, there are several other things worthy of noticing in the advertisements for international relief agencies. For example, poor people are almost always invisible in advertising depicting American society. A simple explanation for this absence is that much advertising is aspirational in that it seeks to provide models to be emulated. Such models are often upscale, and the roles or persons they depict may exceed the social status of the audience to which the advertisements are directed. Another factor that helps explain the absence of poor people in domestic advertising is that their economic deprivation means that they are a segment of the market with severely limited buying power. Thus advertising directed to poor people and reflecting their life circumstances is illogical for both these reasons. More important, however, may be that it is easier to show poor people in other parts of the world because such depictions are consonant with our understanding of our relationship to such people. We are rich; they are poor. We are dominant; they are subordinate. They depend on us for assistance; we are in positions to decide whether to give or to withhold.

In addition, this advertising commodifies children in strictest terms. What is to be bought here is a child, a relationship. The advertisements offer choices of country and sex—not unlike choices of model and color that are features of automobile advertising. Once selected, the child (or the agency acting on the child's behalf) will provide a history, a photograph, and occasional letters. The child is the commodity. Our consumer orientation extends beyond automobiles and luxury items to include children who, for a price, can be acquired.

Contemporary American print advertisements thus show many continuities in the patterns of representing foreigners. Familiar images of otherness reappear as though copied from earlier advertisements. Social relationships depicted in the advertisements instruct readers in the appropriate activities for Americans and for foreigners. Finally, the relationships are not equal and reciprocal. Rather, they are unequal and hierarchical. Thus the veneer in current advertisements differs from those of earlier decades of the twentieth century, but the deeper social and cultural information that they communicate is remarkably consistent across time.

Bibliographic Notes

Gender depiction in American advertisements is the subject of Erving Goffman's *Gender Advertisements* (New York: Harper and Row, 1976). Diane Barthel's *Putting on Appearances: Gender and Advertising* (Philadelphia: Temple University Press, 1988), and Carol Moog's *"Are They Selling Her Lips?" Advertising and Identity* (New York: Morrow, 1990). Barthel's work contains a large number of references to other books and articles on this subject. In addition to these published materials, the filmed lectures of Jean Kilbourne, especially *Killing Us Softly* (Cambridge, Mass.: Cambridge Documentary Films, 1979) and *Still Killing Us Softly* (Cambridge, Mass.: Cambridge Documentary Films, 1987), focus on gender representations in contemporary advertisements.

The concept of Orientalism entered the social sciences and humanities following the publication of Edward Said's *Orientalism* (New York: Pantheon) in 1978. Although his original analysis focused primarily on Orientalism in the academy, the term is widely used today to refer to similar processes in popular culture.

Judith Williamson, in her film *A Sign Is a Fine Investment* (London: Arts Council of Great Britain, 1983), has noted that English advertisements more frequently display foreigners working than they do native English people. Roland Marchand discusses the representation of work in world fairs and expositions in his essay "Corporate Imagery and Popular Education: World's Fairs and Expositions in the United States, 1893–1940," in David E. Nye and Carl Pedersen, eds., *Consumption and American Culture* (Amsterdam: V. U. University Press, 1991).

The representation of the indigenous cultures of the South Pacific in the Polynesian Cultural Center is the subject of Max E. Stanton's chapter, "The Polynesian Cultural Center: A Multi-Ethnic Model of Seven Pacific Cultures," in Valene L. Smith's *Hosts and Guests: The Anthropology of Tourism* (Philadelphia: University of Pennsylvania Press, 1989).

Audience Responses: The Photographs of Tourists

THE ARGUMENT ADVANCED in preceding chapters is that advertisements lay down templates from which Americans construct images of others and judge relations with them. In this brief chapter I ask whether there is any evidence that such messages are actually received, understood, and acted upon by advertising's audience. I consider some possible sources for such evidence.

Representations of others, particularly of foreigners, provide a special opportunity to examine this issue. Many if not most tourists buy souvenirs, send postcards, and take pictures as regular parts of their travels. Their photographs constitute a visual record that may confirm a correspondence between the templates suggested in advertisements and the images and relationships preserved on film.

During a recent semester I asked students at Duke University to examine travel photographs as evidence of this correspondence. The assignment was to select families who would allow us to study their travel photographs. These could be the students' own families or others to whom a certain degree of anonymity could be granted or families whose albums are preserved in libraries or museums.

Experimental Results

What the Duke students found as a result of their research was confirmation of our suspicions about the relation between advertisements and travel photographs. They found that tourists seek out not the Japanese but the Japanesy, and they photograph it. These iconographic representations of otherness—whether Geisha girls and pagodas, San Blas women sewing *molas,* or peasants picking coffee beans—validate expectations about what is to be seen. What would Egypt be without the pyramids, London without the House of Parliament, or Sydney without its opera house? Photographic trophies of tourists standing in front of such sights seem to be essential objectives of modern travel to foreign destinations. These photographs verify that the tourist went, saw, and captured the experience on film.

We also found that the photographic collections contain pictures of native peoples doing whatever it is that they do in the part of the world the tourist visited. Finding them and photographing them in such settings—a Dutch girl walking in wooden shoes, a Moroccan charming a snake, a South Seas islander clutching a spear—also seems to be a part of the photographic record tourists seek to construct. Some of the photographs also show the natives and tourists in the same pictures. And like the patterns in the advertisements, these relations are hierarchical. The tourists are photographed with their favorite guides, bargaining for souvenirs in native markets, or sipping drinks they did not mix. Sometimes the photographs show visitors entangled with people who live in foreign places, but these are usually exceptional situations in which deeper relationships such a studying abroad or visiting one's ancestral homeland underlie the differences.

Reorienting the Study of Travel Photographs

When I first conceived of this chapter, I planned to report on the study of the travel photographs of a few families. I expected that as long as I included enough details about the families, their socioeconomic circumstances, and their travel destinations, it would not make much difference which ones I selected. A necessarily more superficial survey of a large number of families seemed less promising than a more intensive investigation of a few families. The research was begun, and the results it produced further confirmed expectations about what travel photographs would show. The families' photographs showed remarkable similarity to the models in the advertisements. Those who had gone to France had taken photographs of family members with the Eiffel Tower or Notre Dame in the background. Those who had made it to Pisa had photographed themselves near the famous Leaning Tower. In England the families appeared with backdrops of Tower Bridge, Big Ben, or the Houses of Parliament; many had also attempted to get a beefeater guardsman in their picture of at least one family member taken in front of Buckingham Palace. Those who had gone to more exotic settings sought out the equivalent local sights. There were scenes of beaches, visits to ancient ruins, and some native dances or other ceremonies in locales where they could be found.

I began to examine my own reactions to other people's travel photographs to see what I might learn about why viewing them is often a dreaded experience that people typically seek to avoid. In doing so, I came to understand that this response to travel pictures is almost as much a part of American culture as the themes portrayed in the photographs themselves. However, I need not report my own reactions to other people's photographs and slides to occasion understanding in the reader. This experience is so common that the exercise can easily, and

perhaps more profitably, be repeated by each reader, who can then examine his or her own reactions. By directly examining the photographic evidence of tourists depicting other people and places along lines suggested by advertisements, the reader can decide how closely the two correspond.

Other People's Travel Photographs

Any number of acquaintances will happily oblige in this investigation. Since most of us avoid looking at other people's travel photographs, an expression of interest will probably gain entree. However, unlike the people we visit in other parts of the world, these are likely to be your friends. It would be wise to keep the nature of your relationship to them in mind as you peer into their albums and examine their travel trophies with covert motives. Ask, when you do this, whether your responsibility to those who let you enter their private worlds in this way is different from the responsibility you would have to someone whose life you might intrude upon in some foreign touristic destination. You will quickly realize that one major difference is that you, like Lisl Dennis, will probably never again see the little boy sitting in the St. Lucian doorway or the Haitian woman carrying the market basket on her head. Those encounters were brief and specific, but when close acquaintances welcome you into their homes and open up the records of their lives, the encounters are not likely to be superficial. Thus your study of their photographs must be done with care, concern, and some compassion. Its purpose is not to humiliate, to set straight, or to belittle their efforts. It is to understand the nature of photography as artifact.

An evening spent with friends to see the slides of their most recent trip may provide enough evidence to convince you about the degree to which patterns in advertisements are reflected in travel photographs. Here are some questions to guide your research:

1. How do tourists report their travels? Is their account a monologue or some jointly produced story where your questions and comments guide and influence what is said?

2. What order is imposed (or not imposed)? Are slides or photographs merely fetched from a box in no particular order such that each one evokes its own story? Or is there some narrative structure that organizes the presentation? Is order imposed by chronology or geography? Why is no other logic followed (such as one of similarity, say of clouds, doorways, flowers, or some other principle of order)?

3. Is the absence of an opportunity to tell about your travels at the heart of why you may not like seeing slides of someone else's trip? Would the experience be different if you were to take turns showing travel slides?

4. Do the pictures reflect an aesthetic of beauty, typicality, or strangeness, or an ideology of inequality in social relations? Why does the ordinary seem to be underemphasized? Why do the pictures focus on differences in cultures rather than similarities and common themes in human experience?

5. Whom did the photographer have in mind as the intended audience for the travel photographs? Were they taken by a tourist as a travel diary? If so, were they meant as more than a memory aid for the photographer? To what degree is looking at someone's slides or photographs, especially when we do so as an unexpected or unintended audience, like reading someone's diary without permission? Alternatively, how does the experience differ when the photographer constructed a visual record of travel with the intention of later finding an audience for it?

6. Do other people's travel photographs provide an additional model for our own? How many other devices generate our pretravel expectations?

Image/Relationship/Power

These questions may not fit all circumstances, but they can serve as a guide to the issues worthy of examination. What such an exercise is likely to reveal is that the travel slide show replicates many of the issues in the three-step paradigm of image, relationship, and power useful in examining depictions of social relationships in advertisements.

For example, we see the travelers (but not ourselves) shopping, sitting beside monuments, and gazing at touristic sights in foreign settings. We see them dressed in traveling clothes such as safari jackets, new bathing suits, and ski jackets that were perhaps bought especially for the trip. We see the scenery and the physical environment that surrounded them—Greek islands, Red Square, the Grand Canyon, the Taj Mahal, or the Ginza.

In their photographs we also see the natives, doing quaint native things. Gondoliers maneuver boats through Venetian canals, flamenco dancers pose with guitarists in Seville, Maasai warriors walk beside rural roads in Kenya, and craftsmen make carvings in Papua New Guinea. The travelers explain to us how they came to take the particular photographs and what the natives are doing in the pictures they show us.

The slide show demonstrates the status difference between those who travel and those who do not. The narrative that unfolds through pictures and accompanying explanations is also about power and inequality. As we watch, we are continually reminded that we did not go but that the travelers did. When we object—either by attempting to find a means of not accepting invitations to travel slide shows or by trying to bring such evenings to early ends—we do so not to the sights we see in the photographs but to the perpetration of relationships of status inequality. Our complaints and our distaste for the experience, if we listen to ourselves, are couched in the language of rebellion.

As we develop an understanding of all that may be seen in the photographic records of travel, we come to ask: Where are the voices of those whom we colonize through our photographs? Are there only silent images, muzzled by technology and linguistic differences? Have they no voices? Is there no one speaking for them?

Cannibal Tours

A 1987 film about the touristic experience by the Australian filmmaker Dennis O'Rourke provides insight into the reactions of Sepik River villagers to

Western visitors. In popular imagination Papua New Guinea remains one of the outposts of the unconquered primitive world. Most people know that these are not really untouched, pristine cultures because it is now possible to visit them while cruising the river in a luxury ship from which tourists gawk and occasionally wander onto shore. In fantasy and imagination, these Sepik River villages come as close as any to meeting expectations of a contemporary encounter with otherness.

O'Rourke's photographic essay examines the relationships of the visitors with the visited. His photographs are of tourists collecting their own photographic trophies. He asks them about their objectives and motives in traveling and intermingles their responses with villagers' commentaries about the tourists. *Cannibal Tours* produces uncomfortable reactions in many who see it because it treats the tourist, rather than the native, as the object of inquiry. In doing so, it requires its audience to think about what they take pictures of, how they represent the people they photograph as tourists, about responsibilities and relationships they have toward the visited, and about the inequality that typically pervades such relationships.

Photographs as Evidence

The exercise proposed in this chapter allows us to make our own decision about the degree of congruence between the models advertisements provide and touristic practices. The advertising industry most commonly interprets any congruence between advertising representations and social behavior as evidence that advertising mirrors society.

Although this is surely true to some degree, how is it possible to deny that the representational process also provides in each reflection a new model for future behavior?

Contemporary Americans are relatively sophisticated in their expectations about tourism. Such late twentieth-century encounters with other peoples and cultures bear little relationship to Boorstin's characterization of travel two centuries ago. Additionally, they bear only limited similarity to travel and tourism in the early decades of this century. Advertising may now play less of an instructive role than it did in 1929, when it had more opportunity to introduce new practices. Interesting though differences between the two periods may be, too much attention on difference deflects our focus on the regenerative process at work in advertising. Once practices are institutionalized within culture, any effort to disentangle representation and practice in order to assign one primacy oversimplifies the complex interaction between the two.

Bibliographic Notes

Richard Chalfen's *Snapshot Versions of Life* (Bowling Green, Ohio: Bowling Green State University Popular Press, 1987) is a comprehensive study of the role of photography in everyday life. Chapter 5 of his book deals with tourist photography. Susan Stewart's *On Longing: Narratives of the Miniature, the Gigantic, the Souvenir, the Collection* (Baltimore: Johns Hopkins University Press, 1984), especially the portion of the book dealing with souvenirs, is useful further reading on tourist pictures. Those interested in the meaning of photographs and their place in our lives may wish to begin their reading in this complex area with Susan Sontag's *On Photography* (New York: Farrar, Straus, and Giroux, 1977).

6

An Exposition of Twentieth-Century Print Advertisements: Depictions of African Americans

IMAGINE THAT YOU have entered a large museum devoted to the study of advertising. Within its monumental walls are several floors, each having many galleries devoted to specific topics. The museum's collection is so large that only a small proportion of it can be displayed at once. From time to time, the museum mounts special exhibitions such as its current retrospective on "African Americans in American Advertising: A Twentieth-Century Retrospective." This chapter contains a visitor's guide to this hypothetical exhibition.

As in many exhibitions, these individual pieces are stripped from their original contexts. As actual advertisements, each one competed for a reader's attention along with the articles, editorials, cartoons, stories, and other advertisements that filled the pages of the newspapers and magazines where they appeared.

We can never know how much notice the advertisements previously attracted. When they first appeared, they may have been passed over without comment, or they may have occasioned lengthy discussions. What we do know is that these images, and many others like them, have been a constituent part of the discourse about blackness and whiteness, about race and social status, and about inequality in America.

These advertisements record the conventions for depicting African Americans in the context of American society over the twentieth century. Many

seem utterly anachronistic today. They could not and would not appear in contemporary publications. But what seems unthinkable in the contemporary context was conventional just a few decades ago.

In this exhibition the advertisements are displayed against stark white walls as opposed to backgrounds of newsprint or magazine pages that might more faithfully reflect their original contexts. Recognizing that context can never be fully reproduced, the curators have chosen to display these depictions of African Americans against a larger background of whiteness. When seen as a stream of images spanning the century, African Americans stand out as different, as divergent, and as other.

For much of the century, this group of Americans were defined as outside the intended audience for most advertisements. Thus their images could be appropriated and used without much concern for what, if anything, they might think about such representations. However, the civil rights movement brought about many changes in American society, including economic changes that resulted in the increased purchasing power of African Americans in the marketplace. Business, quick to realize the potential of this emergent market, redefined the intended audience for advertisements to include them. Additionally, specialized advertisements promoting goods and services to African-American audiences proliferated in magazines like *Ebony* and

Jet as well as on neighborhood billboards. This expansion of the market resulted in the inclusion of African Americans within the intended audiences for American advertising. And this inclusion meant that the old representational codes would no longer be acceptable.

In the pages that follow, the reader will notice a progression from the early decades of the century, when watermelons and bandanas were icons of the African-American experience, to more recent ones, when advertising makes a greater effort to be inclusive. Prior to the civil rights movement, African Americans were nearly always depicted in inferior or service positions. Nowadays they can sometimes be found in positions that are even higher in status than those occupied by white people who appear in the same advertisement.

Is contemporary advertising therefore nonracist? It is probably more correct to note simply that the representational code has changed since the 1960s than it would be to attempt to answer so complex a question. There is plenty of evidence in the advertisements in this exhibition to debate this. For example, it is less common today to find African-American men shown in service positions, although this does continue. Current depictions are more likely to show them as sports figures (preferring basketballs to tennis rackets) or musicians (playing jazz rather than classical music). Occasionally they appear in business suits sitting behind desks. Is this an adequate reflection of society? Or is it merely the emergence of new stereotypes?

The reader of the catalog can simulate the experience of walking through the galleries by exploring the representations of African Americans in the advertisements reproduced on the following pates. The interpretive notes may be ignored in favor of self-guided exploration and study. I invite the reader's own annotations to complement, correct, or replace the interpretive guide notes. In the end the meaning of an advertisement is what each reader thinks it to be. Nothing more. Nothing less.

Many of the advertisements in this exhibition were selected from the collections of the Balch Institute for Ethnic Studies in Philadelphia. In 1984 the institute mounted its own exhibition "Ethnic Images in Advertising," which was cosponsored by the Anti-Defamation League of B'nai B'rith. This exhibition drew samples from a wide variety of advertising materials, including advertising trade cards, print advertisements, and product packaging. It did not limit itself to any particular ethnic groups; rather, it attempted to consider all groups within America. In addition to the collections from the Balch Institute, the materials in this exhibition were supplemented by print advertisements from a variety of popular magazines published in the late 1980s and 1990s. The interpretive notes give the best available date and the place where each advertisement originally appeared.

Bibliographic Notes

Two places to begin reading about African Americans in advertising are the exhibition catalog entitled *Ethnic Images in Advertising* (Philadelphia: Balch Institute for Ethnic Studies, 1984) and Jan P. Nederveen Pieterse, *White on Black: Images of Africa and Blacks in Western Popular Culture* (New Haven: Yale University Press, 1992).

Interpretive Notes

Figure 6.1. *From an early twentieth-century calendar. (Balch Institute for Ethnic Studies Collection, Philadelphia. Early twentieth century.)*

Figure 6.2. *Before the civil rights movement, African Americans and watermelons appeared together on postcards, in advertising, and in other popular cultural images. The copy explains how the boy pictured in the advertisement is the beneficiary of the scientific knowledge created in Shell research laboratories and dispensed by Shell men to farmers.* (Fortune, *July 1941. Black and white.)*

Figure 6.3. *The connection of the watermelon imagery to the advertised goods or services is often tangential at best. In this particular advertisement, a white man's hand holds a spark plug and checks out its "inside story." This is compared visually to the African-American boy examining the inside of a watermelon. Perhaps an eye-catcher, the link between spark plugs and African Americans is gratuitous.* (Collier's Weekly, *September 20, 1941. Black, white, and red.)*

Figure 6.4. *Perhaps no image more powerfully depicts African-American oppression than the picking of cotton. Although this advertisement appeared many decades after the abolition of slavery, the economic dependency of African Americans on white landowners and manufacturers continued. African-American speech in advertisements was often rendered in dialect, as in this instance.* (Fortune, *February 1941. Full color.)*

Figure 6.5. *Like foreigners, African Americans were usually depicted in the pre–civil rights decades of the twentieth century as workers. Here men, women, and children labor together in the cotton fields to pick the raw material out of which bond paper will be made. African Americans as consumers, especially in publications directed to general audiences, did not appear until the latter decades of this century.* (Fortune, *February 1941. Full color.)*

Figure 6.6. *From the earliest decades of the century, the Rastus character whose face appears even today on boxes of Cream of Wheat was perhaps the best-known African-American man in America. Despite his notoriety, Rastus was only a servant. His authority did not extend beyond knowing how to cater to the tastes of other (usually white) people.* (National Geographic, *May 1918. Black and white.)*

Figure 6.7. *Along with the waiter, another common role for the African-American man was the porter. Here the social inferiority of the porter is depicted by his posture, his uniform, and his language. By contrast, the white man whose luggage is being carried wears a suit and topcoat. The newspaper under his arm is almost superfluous to remind readers of differences in access to education and hence literacy between the two men.* (Fortune, *March 1938. Black and white.)*

Figure 6.8. *Only the recurrence of imagery convinces us that advertising is a discourse that repeats themes about social practices and cultural values. It is this repetition that convinces us of the correctness and familiarity of the images and relationships that appear in advertisements. The African-American man as waiter and porter is common up to the period of the civil rights movement. Not only do these men bend and stoop, but they are usually depicted as physically smaller than those they serve.* (Fortune, *November 1936. Black and white.)*

Figure 6.9. *The African-American dialect is another motif in the advertisements of the pre–civil rights decades. In this instance the short copy reports the room service order issued by the unpictured but presumably white people to whom the beer is being delivered. The copy reveals that the African-American bellhop approves of their brand choice. Both his apparent delight and the words he utters also convey this message. His feelings are derivative, based on vicarious pleasure. There is no hint in advertisements like these that African Americans might have aspirations beyond service occupations.* (Fortune, *November 1936. Black and white.)*

Figure 6.10.   *Machinery is too much for the shoe shine man whose occupational work really does not necessitate mechanization. By contrast, there are businesses that do need and use machines to assist in getting the job done. Perhaps the man whose shoes Sam is shining uses them in his own business.* (Fortune, *October 1940. Black and white.)*

Figure 6.11.   *This formally dressed man is a butler in someone else's home. This 1955 depiction was uncommon just a few years later.* (Time, *April 11, 1955. Black and white.)*

Figure 6.12.   *Another traditional service occupation for African-American men was that of railroad attendant. When air travel was ushered in during the 1960s, African-American men were replaced as attendants by young white women who were originally required to meet strict standards of height, weight, and attractiveness.* (Time, *September 12, 1960. Black and white.)*

Figure 6.13.   *Representations of African-American women in advertisements predating the civil rights movement parallel those of African-American men. This image of an African-American woman whose head is wrapped in a bandana appeared on a brand label for Florida citrus fruit. (Circa 1940s or 1950s. Full color.)*

Figure 6.14.   *Perhaps the best known of the images of African-American women in American advertising is Aunt Jemima. This advertisement from 1920 depicts Aunt Jemima preparing pancakes for a hungry throng of white people. In more recent years, Aunt Jemima has been transformed into a slimmer figure without the large bandana. The dialect has disappeared from advertising copy.* (Saturday Evening Post, *April 10, 1920. Black and white.)*

Figure 6.15.   *African-American women as servants in white families are a recurrent theme in the advertisements of the first half of the twentieth century. In this advertisement from 1941, the African-American maid marvels at the latest-model refrigerator that functions so quietly.* (Collier's Weekly, *May 10, 1941. Black and white.)*

Figure 6.16.   *The notion that African-American women are cooks appears in advertisements having nothing to do with their domestic work. In this advertisement the idea of a cook and her recipe is appropriated and used metaphorically to emphasize the sponsor's "red-hot recipe" for manufacturing railway cars.* (Fortune, *July 1956. Full color.)*

Figure 6.17.   *Many advertisements explicitly depict the structural relationship between African Americans and whites. In this advertisement the same African-American butler who appeared alone in Figure 6.11 is shown pouring a drink for a white man. The caption reflects the status differences by referring to the butler by his first name in contrast to both first and last name for the white man. The copy beneath explains that the white man is also an actor who frequently plays the role of butler; the text even gives the full name of the African-American man.* (Time, *June 6, 1955. Black and white.)*

Figure 6.18.   *Some visual representations depict the relations between African Americans and whites explicitly. In this instance the brand name for California produce incorporates the imagery of African-American men as servants. This label appeared on shipping crates and advertised the freshness of the contents. (Collection of the Balch Institute for Ethnic Studies, Philadelphia. Circa 1950. Full color.)*

Figure 6.19.   *In this advertisement for rail travel, the white passengers are shown as beneficiaries of the service of African-American waiters.* (Time, *September 19, 1955.)*

Figure 6.20.   *The difficulty of fitting tourists into Washington is compared to the ease of packing belongings into a suitcase. The two men in the advertisement are not only different racially but in their attire and work. Note also the differences in facial expressions.* (Fortune, *June 1942. Black and white.)*

Figure 6.21.   *In this wartime advertisement, the rail company apologizes to travelers for inconveniences (like upper berths and coach seats) necessitated by national priorities. "He who 'steps up' also serves" compares the patriotic service of soldiers to that of members of the public who must also make sacrifices in time of war. The other service role—that of the African-American porter—goes unmentioned.* (Fortune, *June 1942. Black and white.)*

Figure 6.22. *White golfers relax in a mountain resort. An African-American uniformed attendant stands ready to hand them towels and shoes in the locker room. He is not a part of their conversation or social interaction. (Fortune, August 1935. Black, white, and sepia.)*

Figure 6.23. *The perplexed white woman in the top picture shies away from the African-American porter until she solves the problem on her own. No longer embarrassed, she stands proud and carries her own luggage. This self-reliance is not treated by the African-American man as taking away from his income earned through tips. Rather, he is depicted as delighted that she no longer needs his help to carry a heavy suitcase. (Fortune, March 1947. Full color.)*

Figure 6.24. *Images of the Old South are appropriated for twentieth-century advertisements. Although we notice that "Toby" is not a slave, his job is one of fetching things. This kind of imagery is especially common in advertisements for American whiskey. (Fortune, July 1935. Full color.)*

Figure 6.25. *The genteel white people at this summer party are served by a happy-to-oblige African-American waiter. (Collier's Weekly, October 11, 1941. Full color.)*

Figure 6.26. *In this advertisement that shows both an African-American man and woman interacting, the subject matter is their service roles. Their conversation, reported here, takes place in dialect. (Saturday Evening Post, July 1, 1940. Black and white.)*

Figure 6.27. *A great transformation took place in the representation of African Americans in the advertisements of the 1960s. The bus, site of Rosa Parks's momentous protest over the discriminatory treatment of African Americans, is the subject of this advertisement. Here the central characters are black, and they do not sit in the back of the bus. However, this advertisement was not directed toward the American public in general but to the readers of* Ebony. *(Ebony, March 1969. Black and white.)*

Figure 6.28. *An African-American career woman, cited here as an authority on energy management, stands in marked contrast to her predecessors in the earlier decades of the twentieth century. (Ebony, August 1982. Black and white.)*

Figure 6.29. *African-American women are almost never depicted as domestic servants in contemporary advertisements. Rather, they appear in a variety of roles that show them in more favorable light and reflect the higher-status positions that some have been able to achieve since the 1960s. This one appeared in a magazine for a general audience rather than one directed primarily to African-American readers. (Time, February 19, 1990. Full color.)*

Figure 6.30. *Advertisements for hair straightening and other ways to emulate whites frequently appeared in African-American–oriented magazines both in the pre–civil rights decades of this century and more recently. (Ebony, November 1968. Black and white.)*

Figure 6.31. *The style and beauty of African-American women are the subjects of many contemporary advertisements. However, such advertisements typically appear in magazines directed mainly to African-American rather than general audiences. (Ebony, June 1992. Full color.)*

Figure 6.32. *African-American men make up a larger portion of U.S. military personnel than they represent in the population at large. Consequently, many recruiting advertisements depict African-American men pursuing military careers. These advertisements tend to emphasize the skills and training they will receive while in military service. (Circa 1990. Full color.)*

Figure 6.33. *African-American executives do appear in some advertisements such as this one. However, African-American role models as successful businessmen are not a common theme in advertisements in general-audience magazines. (Life, October 6, 1972. Full color.)*

Figure 6.34. *African-American men as athletes are a frequent theme in contemporary advertising. This reflects the fact that opportunities to excel in this area have been more available to African Americans than opportunities in other fields. Depictions of such excellence by African Americans tend to be limited to sports that are associated with brute force rather than intellectual skills. (Sports Illustrated, circa 1990. Full color.)*

Figure 6.35. *This scene of urban African Americans on a basketball court fits popular notions about how such people occupy their time. (Fortune, April 24, 1989. Full color.)*

Figure 6.36. *Another familiar depiction of African Americans is as musicians. This one appeared in a magazine intended for an African-American audience. (Essence, December 1992. Full color.)*

Figure 6.37. *Advertising depicting successful African-American men and women began to appear in general-audience magazines in the 1980s. Many campaigns run advertisements with white models in general-audience publications; the same advertisements may be redone with African-American or Hispanic models for publications directed to "ethnic" audiences. When this happens, the so-called ethnic audiences often see both the specialized and general-audience versions. (Time, December 28, 1983. Full color.)*

Figure 6.38. *This advertisement from the 1980s was shot in multiple versions with white, African-American, and Hispanic models for different audiences. (Ebony, December 1983. Full color.)*

Figure 6.39. *Some advertisements now show African-American individuals and families in contexts where only whites would have appeared in pre–civil rights decades. This advertisement for breakfast food could easily apply to any mother and child. (Essence, December 1992. Full color.)*

Figure 6.40. *A feature of current advertising is the effort to include ethnic minorities in its portrayals. This advertisement for toothpaste shows an African-American boy as one of three children brushing their teeth. (Circa 1985. Full color.)*

Figure 6.41. *Interest in African heritage as well as pride in African-American culture underlies the ability of marketers to position and sell dolls like Kenya. (Essence, December 1992. Full color.)*

Figure 6.42. *The Esprit Company has pushed the boundaries of racial integration in America by depicting people of many different ethnic backgrounds in a variety of advertisements. However, this degree of intimacy between people of different backgrounds is rare in most current advertising. (Circa 1990. Full color.)*

Figure 6.43. *No single individual symbolizes the changes that have taken place in American society in the twentieth century more than Dr. Martin Luther King, Jr., whose birthday is now a national holiday. (Ebony, January 1992.)*

A Visitor's Guide to African Americans in American Advertising: A Twentieth-Century Retrospective

Figure 6.1

It's Sweeter
BECAUSE OF PETROLEUM

THE good earth holds the key to its own fertility—buried 10,000 feet deep in an oil well.

At Shell's research laboratories, scientists fitted this key to unlock new riches in field and garden. Out of petroleum gas they got ammonia. With this they treated a waste product of the refineries—sulphuric acid—to make ammonium sulphate. And ammonium sulphate combines with the soil to grow sweeter, juicier fruit . . . more luxuriant flowers!

With their chemical magic, these Shell scientists have also found in petroleum a key to synthetic rubber, glycerine, plastics, germicides—even TNT.

These are incidental accomplishments. The "lifework" of these scientists is the constant improvement of Shell fuels and lubricants.

INDUSTRIAL LUBRICATION needs the utmost efforts of these scientists now as never before—for industrial lubrication sets the pace of production.

Shell's $3,500,000 research facilities, manned by

821 scientists and assistants, exist solely to create something new and better—such as the revolutionary new Shell Turbo Oil. In literally hundreds of instances, Shell lubrication engineers have opened the way to increased production and lower operating costs, by changing lubrication methods.

Before Shell industrial lubricants are offered to you, they are plant-tested under all kinds of actual operating conditions.

With the use of Shell lubricants, you are assured the continued watchfulness of Shell men—a service which needs no prompting. • • •

Are you quite sure that your plant has the benefit of all that is new in lubrication, as it develops? You will find a Shell man's recommendations entirely practical—and made without obligation.

SHELL INDUSTRIAL LUBRICATION

Figure 6.2

it didn't jest grow by itse'f

Cotton doesn't just grow. It must be carefully nurtured in rich soil bountifully supplied with nitrogen, an essential plant food without which growth is impossible.

But nature is often miserly with nitrogen in the soil. She hoards most of her supply in the air. Actually, there is enough nitrogen in the air over one square mile of land to take care of all the earth's needs for ten years.

How to take this nitrogen from the air and put it in the soil—that was a baffling problem. But today chemistry is doing it—and on a grand scale, too! Through a special process perfected by American Cyanamid, nitrogen is lifted right out of the thin air we breathe—and combined with coke and limestone to make the fertilizer *'Aero' Cyanamid*.

And what a fertilizer it is! *'Aero' Cyanamid* not only enriches the soil but sweetens it, assuring finer cotton, better vegetables, fruits, grasslands, sugar cane, corn, wheat and other grains. Every year thousands of tons of this amazing fertilizer flow out of Cyanamid's Niagara Falls Plant to replenish the nitrogen supply of the soil and improve these crops.

Spectacular? Yes, by all measurements and precedents. But it is only one of the numerous ways that Cyanamid, through research and the production of chemicals for thousands of purposes, helps man in his constant effort to improve his living conditions.

American Cyanamid Company

30 ROCKEFELLER PLAZA, NEW YORK, N. Y.

MOLDING THE FUTURE THROUGH CHEMISTRY

Figure 6.4

WHERE *Extra Quality* IN GILBERT PAPER BEGINS

● From sunny southern cotton fields comes much of the strength in Gilbert Quality Papers... the same strength and body which cotton gives to sea-going sails, to workmen's heavy-duty clothes, to ropes, and other fibre products where quality is all-important.

In the production of Gilbert *new-cotton-fibre-content* paper, Gilbert uses selected cloth cuttings from fabric mills. These materials are pure cellulose fibre, full of natural life and strength. They require a minimum of processing, and their vitality imparts to Gilbert papers a distinctive crispness and bank-note crackle.

The *new-cotton-fibre-content* in Gilbert

papers, fortified by the Gilbert process of tub-sizing and air-drying, gives the paper a beautiful, durable finish that withstands erasures and the battering of constant handling. This is an important factor in reducing letterhead and business stationery costs.

In the Gilbert group of *new-cotton-fibre-content* Bonds, Ledgers, Bristols, Onionskins, Vellums and Safety Papers, there are papers that will enhance your company prestige, safeguard values, and encourage efficiency. Write on your business letterhead for a sample portfolio of tub-sized and air-dried Gilbert Quality Papers... then discuss their application to your needs with your printer or Gilbert merchant.

GILBERT
Quality Papers

LANCASTER BOND
100% new-cotton-fibre-content. Made entirely of new, white cuttings. The finest quality, for letterheads of prestige and character.

RESOURCE BOND
50% new-cotton-fibre-content. Made from selected fabric cuttings. The "All-Purpose" bond, for all demands of modern business.

DISPATCH BOND
25% new-cotton-fibre-content. High quality, low cost. Especially suitable to large mailings. Good for office forms and letterheads.

THE GILBERT LINE
includes ledgers and bristols of 100%, 75%, 50%, 25% new-cotton-fibre-content; fine vellum, blue-print, onionskin and safety papers.

THE GILBERT PAPER COMPANY • MENASHA, WISCONSIN, U.S.A.

Figure 6.5

Figure 6.6 • 119

Elevators that have that lazy, uncertain way of getting up and down almost always respond admirably to a program of modernization. Examination usually shows that their basic machinery is sound, but that their *control system* is out of date. Modernize them to *Finger-Tip Control* and they will give the *highest type of modern service.*

Finger-Tip Control, you know, is a very important factor in the field of elevator transportation today. It has placed an entirely new meaning on the word *service.* A large majority of the new Otis installations call for Finger-Tip Control. Fortunately, Finger-Tip Control offers equal opportunities in modernization. Because of it, many elevators can now be modernized where before the cost of modernizing them was almost prohibitive.

Can your elevators be modernized to Finger-Tip Control? How much would be the cost? We'd welcome the opportunity of answering these two questions. No obligation. Otis Elevator Company.

OTIS FINGER-TIP CONTROL
if you want better service

· 115 ·

Figure 6.7

"Yes, suh—Everybody's on the go again"

Business and pleasure are filling faster trains, swifter buses, deluxe ocean liners. Terminals and airports are all a-bustle. Trips and tours make the liveliest social talk these days—America is traveling again!

Your trip, for business or pleasure, will be more exciting...more comfortable...more economical if you stop at the popular N.H.M. hotels in their seven strategic cities. They offer you comfort and conveniences that thrill the most experienced traveler. Delicious food in gay restaurants. Pleasing service that makes you return again and again.

THE "National" HOST

YOU'LL ENJOY THE SERVICE AND ECONOMY OF THESE N.H.M. HOTELS

IN NEW YORK
HOTEL NEW YORKER...Frank L. Andrews, Manager. Connected by private tunnel with Pennsylvania Station. 2500 rooms with tub and shower bath, radio, Servidor, and running ice water. Rates from $3. Garage in connection.

IN NEW YORK
HOTEL LEXINGTON...C. E. Rochester, Manager. 3 blocks from Grand Central Station. 801 cheery rooms, with radio, bath and fmul feather-soft beds. Rates from $3 a day.

IN CINCINNATI
NETHERLAND PLAZA...W. O. Seelbach, Manager. One of America's most beautiful and distinguished hotels. 800 rooms with tub and shower bath, radio, and running ice water. From $3 a day. Garage in hotel building.

IN DETROIT
BOOK-CADILLAC...Darrius Crane, Manager. Rendezvous of Detroit's social and business leaders. 1,200 quiet, beautifully furnished rooms with bath. Rates from $4 a day. Visit the colorful new Esquire Room.

IN CHICAGO
CONGRESS HOTEL...John Burke, Manager. On Michigan Boulevard, overlooking Lake Michigan. Big, comfort-planned rooms, with new furniture and decorations, from $3 a day with bath. Gay new restaurants.

IN DAYTON
HOTEL VAN CLEVE...Richard E. Daley, Manager. Finest hotel in Dayton, with 300 modern, homelike rooms, with bath. From $2.50 a day. New Mayfair Room.

IN DALLAS
HOTEL ADOLPHUS...Fuller Stevens, Manager. The largest hotel in Dallas, 825 rooms with bath. Rates from $2.50 a day. Home of the glamorous new Century Room.

IN MINNEAPOLIS
HOTEL NICOLLET...Neil R. Messick, Manager. Minneapolis' most beautiful hotel, located near railway stations and business center. 600 large, modern rooms. From $2.50, with bath. New Minnesota Terrace and Jolly Miller Cafe.

N.H.M. HOTELS

NATIONAL HOTEL MANAGEMENT CO..INC. RALPH HITZ, President
Washington Office: 986 National Press Building, Metropolitan 3717 · Boston Office: 7 St. James Avenue, Telephone Liberty 1213 · Cleveland Office: 437 Terminal Tower, Telephone Cherry 5126

· 55 ·

Figure 6.8

Figure 6.9

Figure 6.10

7-year-old Walker's DeLuxe makes fine whiskey sours!

As a matter of fact, Walker's DeLuxe makes exceptionally fine drinks of every sort. For it is Hiram Walker's very best bourbon—aged 7 full years in charred oak and elegant in taste. We suggest you order it soon—at your bar, or from your dealer's.

STRAIGHT BOURBON WHISKEY • 7 YEARS OLD • 90.4 PROOF • HIRAM WALKER & SONS INC., PEORIA, ILLINOIS

TIME, APRIL 11, 1955

Where in the world does Northern Pacific find those helpful people who serve you on the Vista-Dome North Coast Limited? No train crew was ever more friendly, quicker to please, more genuinely interested in a passenger's comfort. There's something special about this magnificent train that goes beyond fine food, fine equipment, or even the route that takes you through some of America's finest scenery. It's a happy train with happy people . . . the kind that makes travel <u>fun</u> again!

Where does NP get its financial strength? From oil, timber, real estate, minerals. This substantial non-railroad income enables NP to put more railroad income to work on the railroad. Result: constant improvement of facilities and equipment for shippers and passengers alike. For free copy of travel folder, "Northwest Adventure," write G. W. Rodine, 829 Northern Pacific Railway, St. Paul 1, Minn.

NORTHERN PACIFIC RAILWAY
Route of the Vista-Dome North Coast Limited

TIME, SEPTEMBER 12, 1960

121

Figure 6.12

Figure 6.13

Figure 6.14

127

Mandy's giving us another chance

since we changed to silence!

1 **"I'se quittin'," announces Mandy** heatedly one day last month. "Can't sleep nights on account of the rumbling of that ol' refrigerator. Then just when I'se makin' ice cream, it stops en-tirely!" "John," warns my wife, "if Mandy leaves, we're sunk. We need a new refrigerator . . . *right away!*"

2 **"I know one that can't make a noise,"** she continues. And with that she rushes me downtown to the Servel showroom. There I see a refrigerator . . . *without machinery* . . . with only a tiny gas flame doing the work. Naturally, it's always silent. And having no moving parts, there's nothing to wear.

3 **Among folks who've had experience,** Servel is winning more friends every year. And no wonder. Survey after survey shows that the things people wisely look for in their *second* refrigerator are permanent silence . . . lasting dependability . . . continued low operating cost. And Servel Electrolux is the only automatic that offers all these big advantages.

4 **"Lor-dy, it sure is quiet!"** Mandy's happy and so are we. Servel's saving us enough on food alone to pay the installments. And we always have plenty of ice cubes. "You know," smiles Mandy the other day, "las' place I worked they had one of these gas refrigerators that was 'most ten years old. Looks like me and Servel are goin' to be with you a mighty long time!'"

Stays silent . . . lasts longer

SERVEL
ELECTROLUX
Gas
REFRIGERATOR

FOR FARM AND COUNTRY HOMES—MODELS RUN ON
BOTTLED GAS—TANK GAS—KEROSENE
Write for details to Servel, Inc., Evansville, Ind., or Servel (Canada) Ltd., 457 King St. W., Toronto, Ont.

If you look at <u>one</u> refrigerator, look at Servel—If you look at <u>more</u> than one, look at Servel to see the <u>difference</u>

"We learned from experience that moving parts in a refrigerator can be costly. So there wasn't any question what our new refrigerator would be. We picked a Servel Electrolux and find it very economical."—*Mrs. Stewart W. Tulley, 1812 11th Ave., Sacramento, Cal.*

It freezes with
NO MOVING PARTS! ✓

Figure 6.15

Red-hot recipe for tougher tank cars

WHEN heavy-gauge steel is formed and welded into a tank car tank . . . certain internal stresses develop which tend to weaken the metal. That is why ACF tanks are "popped into the oven" to relieve these stresses.

Each tank is scientifically heated under controlled conditions. This results in a tank of uniform strength which is ready to resist the forces of load and impact which occur during transportation.

When you're looking for the toughest tank cars ever built, look to Shippers'. We are the exclusive sales agent of ACF-DURADOME tank cars for industry. You'll find a nationwide network of Shippers' Car Line offices and repair shops ready to serve your transportation needs.

Whatever your tank car requirements may be, better talk to Shippers' . . . and get the benefits of *modern* tank car service!

Typical DURADOME—designed for formaldehyde service

SHIPPERS' CAR LINE

Division of **acf** INDUSTRIES, Incorporated
30 Church Street, New York 7, N. Y.

CHICAGO, ILL. • HOUSTON, TEX. • SAN FRANCISCO, CAL. • MILTON, PA. • EAST ST. LOUIS, ILL. • SMACKOVER, ARK. • TULSA, OKLA. • NORTH KANSAS CITY, MO. • RED HOUSE, W. VA.

Figure 6.16

Robert thaws out Arthur Treacher

His glacial portrayal of the haughty butler of film comedy has made Arthur Treacher's face familiar to millions—among them, our own real-life Walker's DeLuxe butler, Robert Anthony.

Off-screen, however, Mr. Treacher is a far pleasanter type, as Robert just recently discovered.

During their conversation, Mr. Treacher agreed most affably with all of Robert's expert observations about making guests feel at home—especially when Robert demonstrated one sure way to do this.

Which is, of course, to serve a bourbon whose very excellence will tell your guests how welcome they are.

And for this purpose, you cannot improve on Walker's DeLuxe. It is Hiram Walker's finest bourbon—aged 7 full years in oak, and uncommonly smooth.

We term Walker's DeLuxe the most elegant whiskey you can serve.

And after Mr. Treacher had sampled his highball he said we were well justified in doing so.

We think you'll feel the same way. Why not try Walker's DeLuxe soon?

7-*year-old* Walker's DeLuxe—*the most elegant whiskey you can serve*

STRAIGHT BOURBON WHISKEY • 7 YEARS OLD • 90.4 PROOF • HIRAM WALKER & SONS INC., PEORIA, ILLINOIS

12

TIME, JUNE 6, 1955

Figure 6.17

Figure 6.18 • 131

Figure 6.19

Washington's packing them in!

Too bad Washington can't be packed as skillfully as Hartmann Luggage—there'd be a lot less inconvenience.

Men's Knocabouts 29.50—245.00,   *Bondstreeters* 25.00—270.00

HARTMANN TRUNK COMPANY, RACINE, WISCONSIN

HARTMANN *Luggage*

Figure 6.20

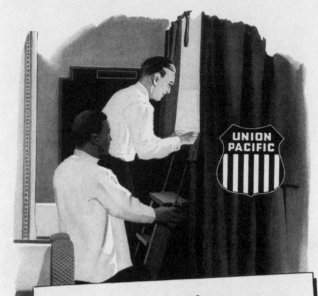

HE WHO "*steps up*" ALSO SERVES

UNION PACIFIC is doing its share to meet the nation's vital need for dependable transportation. It's a job we're proud to do. Over "the strategic middle route" connecting East with West, our gigantic locomotives are hauling not only war materials but also thousands of Uncle Sam's men in uniform.

Thus, it is apparent that travelers may not always find it possible to obtain their preferred accommodations. Perhaps only coach seats or upper berths will be available. To Union Pacific patrons, whom we have had the pleasure of serving and will continue to serve to the best of our ability, we would like to say "he who steps up also serves" and express our thanks for their cooperation.

The Progressive
UNION PACIFIC RAILROAD
The Strategic Middle Route

Figure 6.21

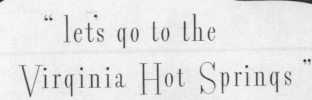

Strange fact that one should go southward to cool off, but fact it is where this resort is concerned. Explanation: for each 300 feet that one travels *upward*, the average temperature drops 1 degree. At the Virginia Hot Springs, U. S. weathermen added the warmest minutes of the warmest hours of the warmest months for 37 years, averaged them, found that August's average was 78.8°, September's 73.6°. Thus, statistically, is corroborated what visitors have known these many years, that summers at The Homestead are delightful . . . It's cool enough for vigorous people to be vigorous, and warm enough for the languid to loll on rolling lawns and watch. At night, there's a pleasant drop to the sixties and fifties, which means the difference between obligation and ecstasy in dancing, with hours of deep sleep to follow . . . But, here we have you tucked in bed and we haven't said a word about golf, or skeet, or tennis, or riding, or even driving a buckboard over the miles of especially maintained dirt roads. If you want to know about the Cascade Course, or the Homestead Course, or the swimming,

it looks as though you will have to ask for our beautiful new portfolio which tells you all about these things. We'll be glad to send it to you and to pay for your telegram of inquiry.

• • •

P. S. *The portfolio also tells about the Homestead Cottages, about the Hot Springs Hydrotherapy Institute, about rates, about ways to get here. It is complete, and we are rather proud of it.*

THE
HOMESTEAD
IN THE COUNTY OF BATH AND THE

STATE OF *Virginia*

ASK FOR THIS BEAUTIFUL PORTFOLIO WHICH DESCRIBES THE HOMESTEAD AND GIVES RATES

Figure 6.22

problem...*

solution

The wear-and-tear of travel is tough on conventional types of luggage. Replacement is costly! For handsome suitcases that can take it, Hercules helped develop a tough, lightweight, colorful material made from fabric laminated with cellulose acetate plastic. It is tougher than steel of equal weight, and lighter than aluminum of equal thickness. Radio cabinets, typewriter cases, and refrigerator panels are just a few other possibilities for this development.

result...

67-2

* TO PRODUCE TOUGH, LIGHTWEIGHT LUGGAGE ... another development utilizing Hercules chemical materials as described in the free book, "A Trip Through Hercules Land."

HERCULES
HERCULES POWDER COMPANY
988 Market Street, Wilmington 99, Delaware

CHEMICAL MATERIALS FOR INDUSTRY

Figure 6.23

Figure 6.24 • 137

At *country club*

...or country store

America's most distinguished beer is waiting for us just about anywhere we ask for it • Some drink it in costly crystal at fashionable country clubs. Some buy it across the counter in friendly country stores • That famous flavor found only in Schlitz knows no class distinction. It's one of life's finer things that everybody can afford. Lovers of good beer the world over ask for Schlitz. There is no substitute for a beer so fine it made a city famous.

America's Most Distinguished Beer

Schlitz

IN BROWN BOTTLES, CANS, AND ON DRAUGHT

THE BEER THAT MADE MILWAUKEE FAMOUS

Copr. 1941, Jos. Schlitz Brewing Company, Milwaukee, Wis.

Figure 6.25

"MAN—YOU SURE ARE CRAZY!"

SELENA: *Here the boss has been givin' you practically new shirts all these years—and you go and spoil it!*

SAM: All I said was, "Boss, how come you don't buy the kind that won't shrink outa size after they're washed?"

SELENA: *Shootin' off your big mouth!*

SAM: And he says, "What kind of shirts? If you mean that pre-shrunk kind, it's no dice!" he says. "Most of them shrink, too."

SELENA: *And plenty!*

SAM: So I says, "No suh, boss. I ain't talkin' about no pre-shrunk shirts. It's *Sanforized-Shrunk* I mean."

"What's the difference?" he says.

"A lot of difference," I tells him. "Don't you ever read the magazines? Seems this Sanforizing process takes all the shrinkin' out of a fabric, down to a measly little ole 1%. And boss," I says, "when a shirt's got the Sanforized-Shrunk label on it, I know it *cain't shrink* out of size."

SELENA: *You know too much—that's your trouble!*

SAM: Right off, the boss wants to know where he can get 'em. "Anywheres," I says. "All the stores sell Sanforized-Shrunk shirts now—most any style or make you want. Don't cost any extra."

SELENA: *Humph! I s'pose you told him where he could get Sanforized shorts and pajamas, too—so you won't get no more of them, either.*

SAM: We-ell, fact is, I did. But listen, Selena! With that, he peels off a wad of bills and tells me to get him a half dozen of everything, and keep the change.

SELENA: *What change? I ain't seen none of it yet.*

SAM: The change is gwine to be on me! Boy, I got me some of the swellest, fanciest Sanforized-Shrunk shirts you ever seen on anybody!

HERE'S YOUR CHANCE, SELENA—

Tell the missus that Sanforizing will end shrinking troubles in everything made of cotton, linen, or spun rayon.

Women's Dresses · Slip Covers & Draperies · Nurses' Uniforms · Children's Clothes · Slacks, Work Clothes

FOR PERMANENT FIT—LOOK FOR THE WORDS—SANFORIZED-SHRUNK

Figure 6.26   •   **139**

Greyhound is for discovering

...missing teeth, mountains, cities,
vacationlands and all the beauty of America.
Low Greyhound fares and fast,
frequent schedules also
make it easy to discover
cousins, aunts, uncles, brothers,
friends and grandmas you
probably haven't seen in years.
We're partial to grandmas.
Take a Greyhound and discover
your grandma, today.

Go Greyhound...and leave the driving to us.

Figure 6.27

People who pour it on

Bobbi Jenine Collins spent a large portion of her childhood in the Watts section of Los Angeles. Her motivation was strong. Strong enough so that she earned a college scholarship. But Bobbi had to wait for college. She wanted to help her family first. That's why she got a job right out of high school.

Jack Tenner, a Los Angeles lawyer, hired her as a legal secretary. She worked for Tenner for five years.

During that time he encouraged her to pursue a law career of her own.

She worked a full day every day. Often with overtime. Then she traveled some twenty miles to classes. Dinner waited till 10:30 or 11:00. And studying came after that. Or on lunch hours. Or weekends.

It took ten years. But she earned her law degree in June, 1965. Early in her career she worked in the law

department at Paramount Studios. In 1967 she got the offer to join Milton A. Rudin, a specialist in entertainment law. Today, Bobbi Jenine Collins is one of three attorneys in the Rudin law offices. Their client list includes some of the most famous names in show business. And she is becoming an expert in a field which has many Negro contributors, but few Negro lawyers.

Figure 6.28

"At first blush, some accounts look just awful. But if you read your D&B right, you can find hope.

"You can see that maybe, if you're patient, you can turn a shaky customer into a great one. "It's the difference between avoiding risk and finding risks worth taking."

Nobody's in business to turn away customers, and that's what makes credit decisions so tricky. As often as possible you want to say yes, but good risks don't always jump out at you.

That's why Dun & Bradstreet offers such depth. Beyond raw numbers, we calculate ratings, indexes and trends. Beyond basic reports, we offer custom formats, analysis, and computer modeling. Beyond how a business runs, we'll give you details about who's running it.

More than any other source, we take you below the surface. Because sometimes, that's where the gold is.

Dun & Bradstreet
The fine art of managing risk.

Dun & Bradstreet Business Credit Services
a company of
The Dun & Bradstreet Corporation

Figure 6.29

HAIR STRATE TURNS HEADS

Soft and swing-y.

Your hair? It can be, with Hair Strate.

Hair Strate is a gentle, no base relaxer that leaves your hair nicer than you've ever imagined.

Down with hair that has a mind of its own! Up with Hair Strate and the hairdo of your choice. Yes, now you can decide what your hair will do, no matter how uncontrollable it has been in the past. Just ask your beautician

for a Hair Strate treatment. And you needn't worry . . . it won't revert.

Soft and swing-y? You decide. Then watch heads turn!

Summit Laboratories, Inc. • P.O. Box 41085 Indianapolis, Indiana 46241

Figure 6.30

Figure 6.31

Figure 6.32

• 145

The phone company wants more executives like Walt Chambers.

Walt Chambers is an Area Commercial Manager for the New Jersey Bell Telephone Company. He is responsible for fourteen telephone business offices handling 350,000 accounts in his home town of Newark and in suburban Essex County.

With the phone company since 1964, Walt has risen fast. "At New Jersey Bell," he says, "we are firmly committed to the practice that all of our employees compete on an equal basis. Our men and women are evaluated and are given chances for advancement or transfer on an equal basis."

And that's the way Walt intends to keep it for the 550 employees he supervises.

That's also the way we want it throughout the Bell System. At whatever level employees enter the company, we want them to do what they like to do and do best. So when openings exist, local Bell Companies are offering applicants and present employees jobs they may not have thought about before.

That's why we have women stringing telephone lines and men working as operators and service representatives.

AT&T and your local Bell Company are equal opportunity employers.

Figure 6.33

Figure 6.34

For Bill Demby, the difference means getting another shot.

When Bill Demby was in Vietnam, he used to dream of coming home and playing a little basketball with the guys.

A dream that all but died when he lost both his legs to a Viet Cong rocket.

But then, a group of researchers discovered that a remarkable DuPont plastic could help make artificial limbs that were more resilient, more flexible, more like life itself.

Thanks to these efforts, Bill Demby is back. And some say, he hasn't lost a step.

At DuPont, we make the things that make a difference.

Better things for better living.

Figure 6.35

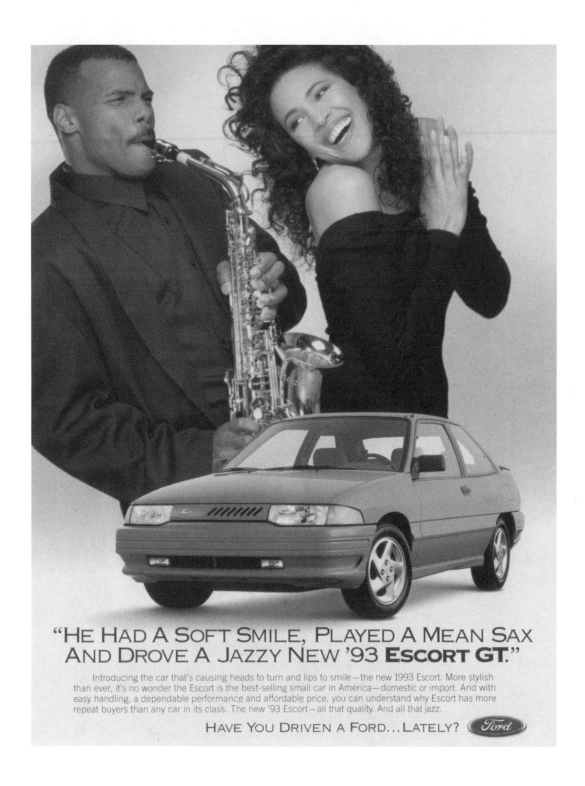

"HE HAD A SOFT SMILE, PLAYED A MEAN SAX AND DROVE A JAZZY NEW '93 **ESCORT GT.**"

Introducing the car that's causing heads to turn and lips to smile—the new 1993 Escort. More stylish than ever, it's no wonder the Escort is the best-selling small car in America—domestic or import. And with easy handling, a dependable performance and affordable price, you can understand why Escort has more repeat buyers than any car in its class. The new '93 Escort—all that quality. And all that jazz.

HAVE YOU DRIVEN A FORD...LATELY?

Figure 6.36

100% NEUTRAL SPIRITS DISTILLED FROM GRAIN. 80 PROOF. GORDON'S DRY GIN CO., LTD., LINDEN, N.J.   © 1983 GORDON'S DRY GIN CO. LTD.

"I could go for something Gordon's"

The possibilities are endless

Figure 6.37

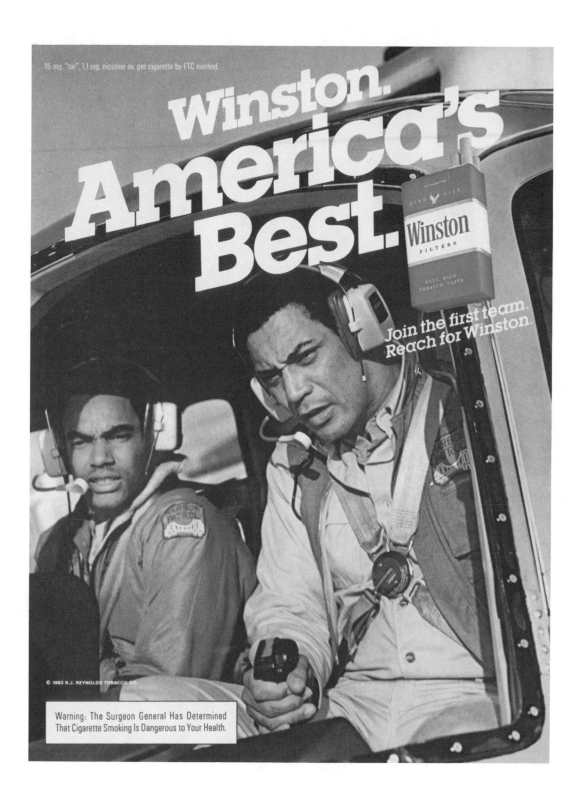

Figure 6.38

152   •

Figure 6.39

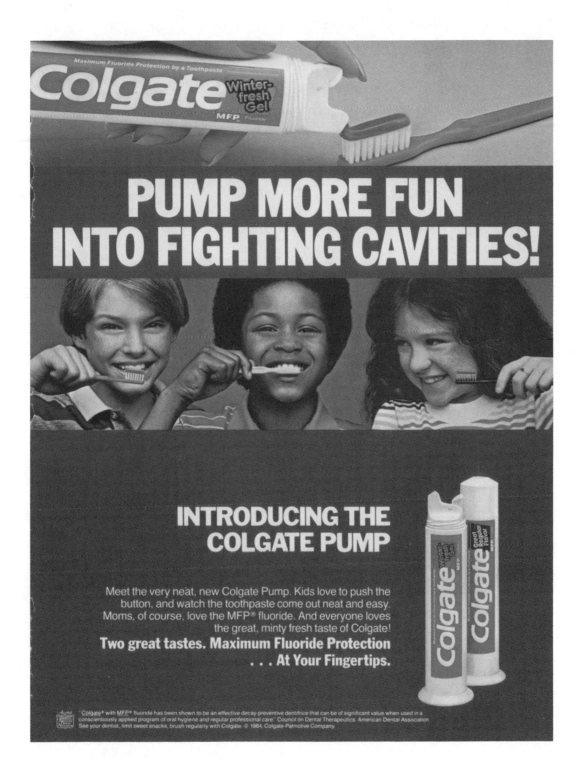

Figure 6.40

Kenya, the doll she'll love for all the right reasons.

CURL IT.

STRAIGHTEN IT.

BRAID IT.

BEAD IT.

Kenya will give your little girl hours of hairstyling fun. She can comb, curl, braid and bead Kenya's beautiful hair, just the way you do hers.

Best of all, Kenya comes in three natural skintones, so your girl is bound to feel pretty and proud. All the reasons why she'll love Kenya.

KENYA
The Beautiful Hairstyling Doll

TYCO ®

© 1992 Tyco Toys, Inc.

154 •

Figure 6.41

Figure 6.42

•   155

It Was Only A Dream,
But It Woke Up The World.

UPI/Bettmann Newsphoto

Over 200,000 people were present when Dr. Martin Luther King, Jr., made his famous March on Washington speech in 1963. Yet his powerful words echoed to millions more around the globe. He described a hopeful vision that "my four little children will one day live in a nation where they will not be judged by the color of their skin but by the content of their character." To him, it was a dream that people of every color, creed and country could believe in. He gave his life trying to make it come true.

We salute Dr. King's work, the hopes that he held, and the things that he stood for. Because at American Airlines, we believe that everyone who has a dream deserves a chance to fulfill it.

AmericanAirlines®
Proud sponsor of the United Negro College Fund.

Figure 6.43

Unexpected Audiences: American and Japanese Representations of One Another

THE EVIDENCE PRESENTED in this book so far suggests that advertising defines and represents much as it pleases, ascribing to itself the specific role of facilitating the promotion of goods and services offered in the marketplace. Advertising claims only to reflect what already exists, not to construct systems of meaning or to create ideological premises on its own. By defining its function so narrowly, advertising pays little or no attention to how its representations are regarded by those who are objectified by it. Advertising considers that it has no essential role in establishing or maintaining a moral order that defines, describes, and even prescribes the culture of its audience. Nor does advertising consider that it sets up a system of contrasts between the culture so defined and the cultures of other peoples and places.

Contemporary advertising does not constitute a single global discourse but rather a set of discourses that operates within the boundaries of nations and languages. Within them, there may also be multiple embedded or overlapping discourses whose intended audiences are based in economic or other internal distinctions. However, each discourse of advertising—whether national or directed to some smaller or larger audience—defines and represents its own categories of self and other, and it has an intended audience whose sensitivities it attempts to respect. It operates without any expectation that those who are defined as outside its

boundaries, that is, who are defined as *other*, may be unexpected audiences. The images and ideas in any discourse of advertising are intended for consumption by specified audiences. How its ideas and images might appear to those on the outside is of little or no consequence.

Genuine shifts in the representational patterns occur only in instances where audiences are redefined to include some who were previously defined as outside. For example, American advertising reconceptualized its representations of African Americans as their status within American society began to change, especially as they became more affluent and thus of greater concern to marketers. Today there is a separate and distinct discourse of advertising directed to African Americans as its specific audience as well as a dominant discourse of American advertising that now considers them a part of its audience. If this were not the case, how could we otherwise account for the changes in the patterns of representing African Americans across the twentieth century?

In future years the globalization of markets may result in changes that will redefine the boundaries of advertising discourses. In the meantime it is worth considering what it is like to be defined as outside an intended audience, especially when that discourse contains representations of one's self and one's culture. To the degree that such understanding is accomplished, we develop an ability to see the world as if we stood in the shoes of those who have been so defined by the discourses with which we are familiar.

In this chapter I examine American and Japanese representations of one another in their respective national advertising discourses. These discourses operate with the expectation that the audiences for the images and ideas about one another are primarily domestic. However, by attempting to view ourselves from a foreign vantage, we increase our empathy for what it is like for those peoples whose cultures have been freely appropriated by twentieth-century American advertising in its promotion of goods and services in the marketplace—a marketplace that also includes ideologies among its offerings.

Shifting Images of the Japanese in American Advertising

The representation of Japan in American advertising has changed considerably over the twentieth century. In the early decades Japan was one of the most exotic foreign countries. In the middle decades of the century, the Japanese became despised enemies. In more recent decades the United States and Japan have become close trading partners. And most recently Japanese success in business has aroused fears that Japan may surpass the United States in industry and technology.

In this section I survey some of the images of Japan that have appeared in the *National Geographic* over the past century. The advertisements in which they appear have focused on Japan as either a trading or business partner or as a tourist destination. In addition to the advertisements in the *National Geographic* that specifically identify Japan, many others refer more generally to the Orient, the Far East, and Asia. These advertisements often include imagery or references that might apply to Japan as well as other East Asian nations.

After centuries of isolation, Japan reopened its ports to foreign ships and established trading relations with Europe and America in the late nineteenth century. A consequence of this opening was broad availability of relatively inexpensive Japanese goods in the American market in the late 1800s and early 1900s. It is this image of Japan that is reflected in a 1914 advertisement for Vantine's Oriental Store in New York City (Figure 7.1). The advertisement explains that Vantine's representatives in the Far East have collected oriental artifacts such as cigarette boxes, dolls, and desk sets that are offered for sale through mail orders. The large illustration at the top of the page shows toy manufacturing in Japan. And for much of the twentieth century, "Made in Japan" signified to Americans inexpensive items of low quality.

The trading partnership between the United States and Japan is discussed further in the advertisements appearing in Figures 7.2 and 7.3. In an advertisement for Waltham watches (Figure 7.2), the company proudly proclaims that the Japanese—having decided to enter the modern world—selected watches of American manufacture over European ones. Despite this bow in the direction of Japan's movement toward modernity, the imagery of the Japanese man in the advertisement is utterly traditional. Moreover, no details are given as to how the Japanese previously reckoned time or the specific uses to which the American watches will be put.

A Western Electric advertisement (Figure 7.3) dealing with raw materials used in the manufacture of telephones mentions Japan as the source for the silk used in telephone cords. The Japanese man is among the most different in appearance from the American man in the advertisement. It is clear visually who is at the center of this trading and manufacturing empire. Taken in tandem, this and the previous advertisement suggest that Japan's economic relation to the United States is both that of producer of raw materials for American manufacturing and consumer of American-made goods.

In Figures 7.4 and 7.5, Japan is depicted as a tourist destination. The images—in pictures and words—portray the exoticism of Japan. Geisha girls, rickshaws, and arched footbridges are typical of the imagery used to evoke and signify Japan in the early decades of the twentieth century.

Figure 7.1

Figure 7.2

These men made your telephone

Japanese. Prepares the silk in the telephone cord.

Irishman raises flax, used in the condenser.

British Indian. A swarthy miner of mica.

Brazilian. He drains rubber from a tree for the receiver.

Russian mines platinum for your telephone.

Egyptian. We must go to the Nile for certain cottons.

Pennsylvanian coal miner. Inside the transmitter are grains of coal.

Alaskan. Your telephone needs gold, too, and here's the man who digs it.

—and the workman at Chicago

HE is one of 28,000 men and women at the Western Electric works in Chicago.

From a slab of rubber, a bundle of vegetable and animal fibers and a curious medley of minerals brought from every corner of the world, this man's skill produces a marvel of precision and ruggedness — your telephone.

Western Electric

Since 1869 Makers of Electrical Equipment

No. 2 of a series on raw materials.

The picturesque types above are gathering some of the materials needed in your telephone.

Figure 7.3   •   161

For those who have traveled!

South America-Africa Cruise

FOR you . . . Canadian Pacific presents the most intriguing of cruises.

On January 21, next, you sail out of New York's winter straight into West Indies' summer. Then . . . Rio de Janeiro . . . Montevideo . . . Buenos Aires . . . gay cities . . . capitals of sister empires. Then . . . startling contrast, the loneliest colony in the world, Tristan da Cunha. Back to up-and-coming cities . . . South Africa. Into the jungle of the ages . . . Victoria Falls . . . Kaffir kraals. A swift curtain . . . Dar-es-Salaam . . . Mombasa . . . blacks and Arabs, Hindus and whites. Finally, back to the start of the world . . . Egypt and the Mediterranean 104 days.

What privileged sights! What odd corners! Yet, never are you without your Canadian Pacific service, your 20th Century comforts, your caviar and camembert.

And your home throughout is the ship of ships for tropical cruise-voyaging, the Duchess of Atholl . . . 20,000 gross tons. Ball-louvre pressure ventilation. A whole deck of stunning, modern-decorated public rooms. Another whole sports deck. And a staff imbued with the spirit of service.

ROUND-THE-WORLD CRUISE

From New York, December 2, 137 days. Empress of Australia, 21,850 gross tons. As low as $2000.

MEDITERRANEAN CRUISES

From New York, Feb. 3, by Empress of Scotland. Feb. 13, by Empress of France. Both 73 days. As low as $900.

The alluring details are in booklets. If you have a good travel-agent, ask him. Information also from any Canadian Pacific office. New York, 344 Madison Ave. . . . Chicago, 71 E. Jackson Blvd. . . . Montreal, 201 St. James St., West . . . and 30 other cities in United States and Canada.

Canadian Pacific
World's Greatest Travel System

Figure 7.4

LAND OF CEREMONY

THE TEA CEREMONY—INTRODUCED BY THE SHOGUN ASHIKAGA YOSHIMASA

THE visitor to Old Japan is always delighted with the gracious ceremonies to which even the simplest acts are elevated. How perfectly this artistic reverence prepares one for the wonders of the Blossom Empire—its mirror lakes and painted valleys, the centuries-old craftsmanship, all the ancient loveliness of shrines and temples.

Most pleasantly surprising is the existence side by side with these ancient beauties of the modern miracles of traveling comfort and convenience. Swift, super-luxury express trains whisk the traveler from city to city. Large, modern hotels await him everywhere with all the familiar facilities and services. Automobiles spin into the remotest sections. Even the favorite sports are amply provided for — golf, tennis, baseball, riding or flying.

The Japan Tourist Bureau (a non-commercial organization) maintains an office in New York in addition to widespread facilities in Japan for the special service of visitors. It will be honored to help plan your itinerary, arrange all the details of accommodations, and serve you while in Japan, without additional cost. It will make your visit to "The All Year Paradise" an unforgettable experience.

The wonderlands of Japan, Korea, Manchuria and China are reached from the United States and Canada by the Nippon Yusen Kaisha, Osaka Shosen Kaisha, the American Mail Line, Canadian Pacific and the Dollar Steamship Line. Full information will be furnished by any of these Lines, any tourist agency, or by the Japan Tourist Bureau.

JAPAN
TOURIST BUREAU
c/o Japanese Gov't Rys., One Madison Ave., N.Y.C.
c/o Nippon Yusen Kaisha, 545 Fifth Ave., N.Y.C.

Figure 7.5 • 163

Together, these images constitute popular notions of Japan.

Around 1930 the Japan Tourist Bureau in New York began placing advertisements encouraging travelers to visit the country. These advertisements, such as the one in Figure 7.5, develop this imagery even more fully than the advertisements produced by cruise lines and tour operators. In this particular advertisement, the traditional cultural practices of Japan are emphasized. In addition to enjoying the ceremonies and arts, the tourist is promised conveniences of comfortable hotels, fast trains, and familiar sporting activities.

This representation of Japan continues in the travel advertising throughout the 1930s. In 1940, just months before the bombing of Pearl Harbor, the two advertisements in Figure 7.6 appeared in the *National Geographic*. They emphasize Japan's natural beauty and rich cultural traditions. The same images that appeared in previous travel advertisements reappear here. Pagodas, kimonos, and Mt. Fuji are familiar icons of Japan.

Such images of Japan as a tourist destination disappeared for nearly two decades; another image of Japan took their place. Although the child is not specifically identified in the Fisher Body advertisement in Figure 7.7, the reader may well imagine that he is Japanese. The more dominating figure of the American soldier along with the might of American-made airplanes suggest American superiority over the childlike Oriental.

Travel promotion for other Asian countries reappeared almost immediately after the end of World War II, but it was not until the 1960s that Japan reappeared as a tourist destination—and as a business partner. The image of the exotic and submissive Oriental women of prewar advertisements is again found in later advertisements for air travel (see Figure 7.8). Japanese men, never powerful in the prewar advertising, cease to be exotic. Rather, they are depicted wearing Western clothes and working in serious business contexts. In the AT&T advertisement (Figure 7.9), the Japanese president of Panasonic expresses admiration for American ingenuity and manufactured goods. This image of

the Japanese man is markedly different from anything that appeared earlier.

In another advertisement for Japan Air Lines (Figure 7.10), mutual respect and admiration are depicted. An American man is shown wearing a Japanese robe and eating sushi with chopsticks while a Japanese man dressed in a business suit eats a steak with Western cutlery. This intermingling of cultures attempts to capture a new relationship between Americans and Japanese. In another JAL advertisement (not reproduced here), the Japanese national airline promises a visit to Japan "where you will meet Orientals instead of look at them."

In a 1980 advertisement for the Bell System (Figure 7.11), an American of Japanese descent is shown making a telephone call to her grandmother in Japan. The dialing codes for more than two dozen cities in Japan are included in the advertisement, which also gives instructions on direct dialing from the United States to Japan. The advertisement emphasizes cultural continuities and similarities of emotions and experience that were not depicted in the representations of Japan in earlier advertisements. Japan's foreignness and former enemy status are replaced here by the treatment of Japan as yet another of the "old countries" for an American ethnic group.

By the 1980s Japanese business success amounted to a new threat to the United States. In the advertisement reproduced in Figure 7.12, an American company directly addresses the issue of Japan's challenge to American industrial superiority. In this first-in-a-series advertisement, the Motorola Company promises to continue dealing with this issue. Many other advertisements as well as articles and books have addressed Japanese business practices and their consequences for America over the past decade.

In the Citicorp advertisement (Figure 7.13), the Japanese have become tourists in America. Here they are shown as camera-carrying businessmen—combining two new stereotypes—visiting the Navajo Indians in the American Southwest. In earlier centuries there were no references whatsoever to the Japanese as tourists or businessmen on a par

Realm of Pageantry

Marked by fascinating festivals...depicted in brilliant pageantry...the twenty-six centuries of Japan's history unfolds this year in spectacular celebration.

Guests, here to enjoy the ceaseless charms of enchanting Nippon, are delighted to find the year-long festivities of 1940 adding extra pleasure to a visit that is always rich in enjoyment...enchanting the magnificent scenic beauty of this flowered land—the spells cast by ancient rites performed in majestic temples and sacred shrines.

Modern accommodations and conveniences ... fine hotels, excellent transportation...Western World pastimes and amusements—all are here to multiply your enjoyment of the vacation that has become the preference of discriminating travelers.

BOARD OF TOURIST INDUSTRY
JAPANESE GOVERNMENT RAILWAYS

For illustrated literature, apply to your travel agent or Japan Tourist Bureau, 630 Fifth Ave., New York, or 1151 S. Broadway, Los Angeles, Calif.

Japan

2600th ANNIVERSARY YEAR — 660 B. C. — 1940 A. D.

"Mention the Geographic

Endless Beauty...
Eternal Serenity

Ageless ... immortal ... the rare loveliness of this enchanting land reflects its lasting image in the wondrous rapture of visitors to Japan.

On every side one finds exquisite beauty revered for more than eighty generations. Blending with these priceless settings of placid lakes, gleaming cascades ...stately, snow-tipped mountains, bounteous gardens, pagodas, arching bridges...are the charming legends, unaltering traditions, fascinating pageantry of ancient Nippon.

Here, Time tells an enthralling story— a tale contrasting strangely with the ultra-modern conveniences and Western World comforts and diversions.

In Japan, visitors live and travel amid every luxury, yet know the rare experience of beauty that is beyond equal... restfulness that is unsurpassed.

BOARD OF TOURIST INDUSTRY
JAPANESE GOVERNMENT RAILWAYS

For illustrated literature, apply to your travel agent or Japan Tourist Bureau, 630 Fifth Ave., New York, or 1151 South Broadway, Los Angeles.

Japan

2600th ANNIVERSARY YEAR — 660 B. C. — 1940 A. D.

"Mention the Geograph

Figure 7.6

The Army-Navy "E" flies above seven Fisher Body plants for excellence in aircraft production and from two others for tank production, while the Navy "E," with five stars, is flown by still another Fisher Body plant for its naval ordnance work.

STRICTLY SUPER

IT'S a great day for our side whenever our flyers sweep out over the target in those fleets of B-29 Superfortresses.

Of course, Fisher Body does not make the complete Superfortress. But it does make huge dorsal fins, horizontal stabilizers, rudders, elevators and ailerons. Yes, and flaps, wing tips, outboard wings and turret parts, too.

More than that, Fisher Body makes engine nacelles—using more than 18,000 jigs and tools to turn out the 3,000 parts that are required for each nacelle.

Fisher Body is proud of its part in building this great Boeing-designed ship. All the skills and techniques inherent in the Fisher Body organization are concentrated on giving superworkmanship to the Superfortress. Yet

it is but one of many war jobs including big guns, delicate aircraft instruments, tanks, and assemblies for other bombers.

And you may be certain that as long as war equipment is needed, the fine craftsmanship symbolized by the "Body by Fisher" emblem will keep right on backing up the courageous crews who pilot these great superplanes.

Every Sunday Afternoon
GENERAL MOTORS SYMPHONY OF THE AIR
NBC Network

armament
B~~ODY~~ BY *Fisher*

DIVISION OF GENERAL MOTORS

Figure 7.7

We're all you expect Japan to be.

Your Japan Air Lines hostess is much more than an airline stewardess. She's an artful conjurer. She brings to life the atmosphere of serenity and peace, of welcome and personal attention, that is Japan at its most charming. It's something you can expect from us, wherever in the world you're heading. For we take the legendary hospitality of Japan...everywhere.

JAPAN AIR LINES

The pleasures of Japan await you around the world. Between 24 countries. 35 cities. For reservations, see JAL or your travel agent.

Figure 7.8

168   •

Figure 7.9

How to Fly, Japanese Style.

One man's <u>sushi</u> is another man's steak.

First Class service aboard Japan Air Lines

There's just no second guessing about taste.
So, to keep everyone happy, we have a simple solution.

Two cuisines.
One is Japanese.
The other is Continental.

No matter which one you choose—the familiar or the adventurous—one thing remains the same: the elegant, understated service that is ours alone.

It's reflected in the smile of your JAL hostess as she offers you a steaming *oshibori* towel to refresh yourself. Her delicate grace as she pours your *sake*. The very special way she makes you feel like an honored guest at a family banquet.

Unique service like this doesn't just happen at mealtime. From our first hello to our last *sayonara*, we do our best to prove there's as much difference between airlines as between airline menus.

We're the one where East meets West.

JAPAN AIR LINES

Figure 7.10

Figure 7.11

Figure 7.12

How we traded with the Navajos.

—Seiko Watch Executives

Seiko in Tokyo knows its executives may end up just about anywhere. So Seiko gives them Citicorp® Travelers Checks to take along to use at hotels, restaurants and for other expenses. Even some personal ones. Like turquoise and ten-gallon hats.

But you don't have to work for Seiko in Tokyo to find that Citicorp Travelers Checks are accepted everywhere you go, even in remote, out of the way places. And that they are refundable in thousands of locations around the world.

So whether you're going on a leisurely vacation to the mountains, or to the land of sandstone and sagebrush, carry Citicorp Travelers Checks. And be prepared for anything.

Because you never know where you might end up.

Figure 7.13

with Americans. They were the visited, never the visitors.

These advertisements, drawn from the pages of the *National Geographic* magazine, briefly chronicle the panorama of images of Japan and its people that have been depicted in the discourse of American advertising in the twentieth century. Taken together, they are a barometer of the changing relations between the two cultures as recorded in the history of advertising. Throughout the century the Japanese have been defined as other in the discourse of American advertising, although the specifics of what this meant have indeed undergone significant changes. There has never been any real expectation that these advertisements were intended for a Japanese audience. Rather, the intended audience for them was always American. For example, what would be the point of advertising to a Japanese audience made-in-Japan curios in 1914 or travel to Japan in 1940? Or in the 1980s could expressions of concern over Japanese industrial superiority possibly be meant for Japanese readers?

Images of America and the West in Contemporary Japanese Print Advertisements

The images of America and the West that appear in contemporary Japanese advertising startle many Westerners when they encounter them for the first time. Their accidental encounter by an American tourist or businessperson on a visit to Japan often evokes surprise, confusion, and misunderstanding. Such encounters were not the ones the makers of the advertisements had in mind when they constructed the images and ideas in the advertisements.

In this section I examine the representation of Americans (and the West more generally) in contemporary Japanese print advertisements. What I experience when studying such advertisements, which are not really intended for me as a part of their audience, are representations of myself and my culture that diverge in many ways from my own

definitions of self. It is this discrepancy in experience that lies at the heart of Edward Said's Orientalism. Such representations are puzzling, often difficult to comprehend, and sometimes enraging. But such reactions are of no consequence to a discourse that defines Western readers as outside its audience.

Although it would be possible and profitable to undertake a study of the representational process since Japan opened its borders to the West in 1868, the differences between contemporary Japanese and Western advertising traditions are so great that their study and comparison constitute a formidable project. The lessons that we learn lay the groundwork for a fuller study of Japanese representations of the West over time as well as for studies of other national advertising discourses and their own depictions of otherness.

The extraordinary number of foreigners appearing in contemporary Japanese advertising is one of its most distinctive features. First-time Western visitors to Japan quickly notice this; even Westerners who have lived there a long time continue to talk about it. But the foreign models do not occasion so much reaction from the Japanese, who are accustomed to it.

Visitors and analysts writing for foreign audiences have attempted to ask why there are so many Western models in Japanese advertisements. A brief review of the history of Japanese relations with the West is helpful in understanding images of the West in contemporary Japanese advertising. To begin, it must be remembered that the relationship of Japan with the West is distinctive among non-Western nations. Japan was never an official colony of any of them. In addition the intrusion of Western culture into Japan was much more controlled than in most other non-Western countries. In 1639 Japan expelled all foreigners, closing itself off from any significant contact with the outside world for more than two centuries.

The policy of self-isolation changed in 1868 with the Meiji restoration. A radical shift in national policy determined that this isolation had left Japan outside the sweep of changes modernizing the world. The Japanese studied the West, translating

Western books and importing Western goods. Westernization was undertaken as vigorously as it had previously been prohibited.

The decades following 1868 were ones of mutual interest and engagement. Japanese aesthetics greatly influenced European artists; Western literature and material culture had their impact on Japan. This intermingling resulted in the development of cultural stereotypes that persist to this day: for Japan, tea houses, serene gardens, paper umbrellas, submissive women, and ferocious warriors; for the West, cultural refinement in music and painting, idealized physical beauty, material abundance, and enjoyment of the good life.

In the early Meiji period, the Japanese image of the West was based primarily on book learning and a small number of investigatory visits to Western countries by members of the Japanese elite. The images that emerged from this kind of contact were highly favorable. They focused on idealized culture and on theory rather than practice. Only later as a result of increased contact did the flaws and failures within the West enter the Japanese understandings of Western otherness. The early romantic bubble burst, the inequities of Western-Japanese trade increased, and a growing sense of nationalism in Japan resulted in a retreat from a respect and reverence for all things Western.

Occupation by the victorious U.S. forces after World War II gave many Japanese a closer look at the powerful Westerners whose military might had put the Japanese to shame. Many Japanese institutions were recast in an American mold, and American culture and values were greatly admired. The postwar period began a new era of Westernization, but it was America, not Europe, that was the specific referent and model for the Japanese.

Immediately following the war, it was out of the question that Japanese could travel abroad. The country was poor, and its people were often hungry. But this did not mean that the Japanese were not exposed to Americans and American culture. In addition to the many Americans stationed in Japan, movies, television, and other forms of popular culture exposed the Japanese to the American life-style.

The representations of American culture occurring in comic strips like "Blondie" and in television programs like "Father Knows Best" greatly influenced the Japanese. Read by the Japanese in this period, "Blondie" depicted the abundance and leisure of the American life-style. One of its most frequently recurring images was Dagwood, relaxing in his overstuffed easy chair in front of the TV. Blondie's kitchen, enormous by Japanese standards, contained an oversized and abundantly stocked refrigerator Dagwood regularly raided to prepare his signature sandwiches. In addition to all these material aspects of American culture depicted in the comic strip, the relationship of the obedient wife to the man as head of the household was not lost on the Japanese audience. Whatever these images may have meant to their native audience, their connotations to the Japanese were probably different. The spaciousness of the middle-class, suburban house and the life-style of its occupants were repeated in "Father Knows Best" and other television programs imported from the United States. The American life-style of the 1950s and 1960s was much admired by the Japanese. It was in many ways a parallel phase to the early fascination with the West following the Meiji restoration.

But things have changed. Japan has become rich; its people travel widely; its technology sets world standards for efficiency and quality. Simple admiration of America has become complicated by more knowledge. Racial tensions, poverty, drugs, and other blemishes of contemporary America are well known to the Japanese today. The material culture once dreamed of—television sets, automobiles, cameras—no longer have their source in the West.

Against this background of prosperity and domestic affluence stands the paradoxical use of Western models and images in Japanese advertising. Goods as diverse as perfume, automobiles, alcoholic beverages, clothing, and electronics are frequently promoted with Western rather than

Japanese models in both contemporary print advertisements and television commercials. Although foreign motifs had been used in earlier decades in association with the promotion of imported goods, the current trend of using Westerners and Western images began following the war. Today it is estimated that as many as a quarter of the models appearing in Japanese advertisements may be Western.

In the years immediately following the war, Western models and images connoted the power and might that had been demonstrated in the war. The West, and America in particular, was held in awe. Western models and images were icons of abundance and success. Beginning in 1970, advertisers began to replace unknown Western models with celebrities. The first of these was Charles Bronson, who endorsed Mandom toiletries for men. He was followed in successive years by a long list that includes Paul Newman, Michael J. Fox, Charlie Sheen, Audrey Hepburn, and Madonna. Advertisements featuring these celebrities are seldom seen outside Japan.

It would be a gross oversimplification of the current situation to say that the use of Western celebrities is an effort to further Westernize Japan. A more correct interpretation would appear to be that in modern, cosmopolitan Japan these celebrities are internationally known figures who happen to be Western. Their use lends a global and up-market quality to the advertisements in which they appear and to the products they endorse.

By contrast, the use of unknown Western models is somewhat more complex. There seems to be a view within Japan that Western clothes often look better on Western models and that products associated with origins abroad keep some of the aura of the exotic by association with foreigners. It is no simple matter, and any effort to provide a unified explanation would not only be simplistic but probably wrong.

Having sketched Japanese history and some key points about marketing within Japan, I turn now to examine what it is within Japanese advertising that has occasioned so much commentary concerning the depictions of foreigners within Japanese advertisements.

An advertisement for the 1990 Audi (not reproduced here) in many ways typifies an advertising style that is much more common in Japan than in most other countries. It is a kind of print advertisement or television commercial that evokes a mood by telling a story or describing a scene or situation. The visual portion and the narrative (if there is one) play roles in the evocation. In the Audi advertisement, a white model looks out over snow-covered mountains. He surveys the snow, trees, and open spaces as he leans on a spotless, shining new Audi 90. The reader cannot tell from the advertisement just what his nationality is or in which country the photograph was taken. A headline reads: "Latitude 43 degrees, 28 minutes North. Longitude East 142 degrees, 27 minutes. I encountered scenery I did not expect." The reader could turn to the globe to determine just where this point on earth is located. (In fact, many Japanese advertisements include references like this that require a bit more work on the part of the audience than do most Western advertisements.) The smaller type in the upper left reads: "Only quality goods from all over the world." The long copy fleshes out the story:

> I remember I was surprised when I first heard that there is an occupation called adventurer, but, come to think of it, we rarely even think about adventures in our daily lives. That's how I feel anyway. Four months ago I decided to go on a little adventure. I managed to take several days off from my busy schedule, and I just headed off on an adventure using only the road map I had and without making any decision about where I would go. It was like a trip back to winter, leaving behind the warmth of the city. Of course I had no hotel reservations. I simply drove and drove. I made some new discoveries, such as what the winter wind feels like and the warm hearts of strangers. Eventually, I found myself in the snow-covered highlands. All I could see was snow and the mountain ranges far away and the sky, but I found myself filled with happiness, happiness that is hard to explain. I forgot all my worldly worries and

was left with awe and excitement. That's the kind of search for truth that I want to experience once in a while. Audi 90: It's a sport saloon [sedan] that satisfies the adventure-minded with its accurate driving.

It is perhaps not so unusual to find a Westerner in association with an automobile imported from a Western country, but how many American advertisements are like this? How often do advertisements for Japanese cars in American magazines show Japanese people driving Japanese cars in their native land?

Despite their seeming omnipresence in Japanese advertisements, Westerners are in fact associated with particular themes or situations. In this instance the Westerner evokes the foreignness of an Audi. There is no practical reason to import foreign cars into one of the world's leading automobile-producing nations. Rather, the Audi signifies the exotic, the imported, the luxurious. A foreign car is simply more expensive than a domestic one. The selling points in the advertisement do not focus on dependability or precision, although the small print details some of the car's specifications.

In addition to luxury, the Audi is associated in the advertisement with freedom of spirit and a relaxation of the many constraints of the workaday life and of the "salary man." Indeed, the story relates the narrator's surprise in learning of "adventurers" and his fantasies of adventure. The contrast is set up between ordered and flexible life-styles. It is in its most basic outline a story about Japan and the West. It contrasts order and freedom, crowded cities and spacious outdoors, us and them.

Figure 7.14 shows unknown Western models demonstrating the ability of the Minolta Alpha-8700i camera to freeze action. The copy (from the bold caption through the fine print) reads:

That split-second feeling—Alpha. It's here! Loaded with high-speed AF and 1/8000 second high-speed shutter. Vividly captures that thrilling moment. High-speed AF, single-lens Minolta Alpha 8700i. Now available. The high-speed AF aligns perfectly in an instant. The super-fast, 1/8000-second shutter

combines with the AF to bring out the beauty of the moment that even the human eye cannot catch. Surprising beauty and breathtaking sharpness. Alpha 8700i lifts you to an all new dimension in the world of photography. The feeling of the moment—now captured forever in the image. The split-second intelligence of Alpha 8700i. With AF and single-lens quality for the '90s. New on the market from Minolta.

The association of Western models with action, freedom, and flexibility is also made in the semiotics of this advertisement. The models might have been Japanese, but they are not. Uses like this one help construct the contrast between Japan and the West, between order and flexibility, between studied behavior and action.

This use of Westerners to signify an alternative to the expectations and conventions of Japanese society is recurrent and telling. It is repeated in the discourse of advertising as well as in the direct imports of Western, especially American, popular culture—films, television, and music. It is also this freedom from the restraints of one's own conventions that constitutes the appeal of Europe and America as tourist destinations for the increasingly affluent Japanese traveling public.

Western society also provides an important model for enjoying the good life. Contemporary Japan is a hardworking, materially successful society. What has not been so clearly developed along with the other changes in postwar Japan is the model for relaxation and enjoyment of the benefits of hard work. In many ways Japan looks to the United States to provide that model.

Figure 7.15, an advertisement for Vogue cigarettes, shows one of a popular series that depicts the American bar scene. The English-language product name, Vogue, a New York club, its address, and opening hour; and the unusual English phrase "Let's clubbing," appear in this advertisement. Such uses of the English language are frequent. Like the Western models, these words and phrases evoke foreignness and sophistication. But the language used in this manner, often strange to the native speaker, is not English but an appropriation of En-

Figure 7.14

178   •

glish. This is not an advertisement whose intended audience will balk at the unusual expressions or find the strange uses of words or phrases out of place. This is an advertisement for Japanese speakers for whom English words and phrases connote another culture and some of its attributes.

The Japanese text explains the picture and the foreign words:

> Work is over. So let's go out on the town and have fun! The first floor is a chic lounge with a Victorian atmosphere. People leaning over their glasses and talking as live jazz music plays in the background. Downstairs, the atmosphere changes. A dance floor with club music blasting. A wave of people dancing like crazy. Both floors coming alive with guests of all nationalities—to be expected in this melting pot of New York. Moreover, the guests are extraordinarily fashionable. And look—in the picture, Elena and Lynn too appear to be enjoying their endless night here at Nell's.

This description of New York nightlife focuses on chicness, frenzied dancing, and cultural mixing. These are Japanese images of the excitement of New York. These attributes of New York are certainly to be found among its many characteristics, but their selection and use in this advertisement tell more about Japan than about New York. Knowing how to have a good time, letting go, and forgetting about what one must remember at home are Japanese fantasies that seem able to be realized in New York. America as a melting pot stands in opposition to Japan, where foreigners, called *gaijin*, are not easily integrated into intimacy. The bold print in the advertisement reads, "The job is done. Let's play. Let's play." This America, then, is a world of dreams.

An advertisement for Asahi beer (Figure 7.16) extols the virtues of a dry beer that originated in Japan. The advertisement claims that the "Karakuchi" flavor is changing the world's taste in beers. The copy reads: "The Japanese have developed a rich and delicious eating tradition. We have aimed to carry on that tradition in beer by bringing out the freshness of beer's natural elements. A re-

fined, clear taste. Drink as many as you can of this beer with a crisp, defined flavor. This new deliciousness is, indeed, a Japanese original. This taste is now changing the trend in beer all around the world."

Several things are worth noting about this advertisement. First, the claim in the copy about Japanese superiority and its effect on beer making around the world should not be overlooked. As a part of its increasing cosmopolitanization, Japan interacts with the rest of the world through imports and exports. In this instance Japanese taste and Japanese standards have had their impact elsewhere. Second, the photograph shows that effect in a distinctly non-Japanese setting—the wide open spaces of the American West. Here in a boat in a river or lake, a Japanese man (or an American of Japanese ancestry?) who is a professor of computer science at an American university enjoys Japanese beer.

Third, this advertisement shows both a Japanese and a Westerner interacting. The presence of both Japanese and non-Japanese in a single advertisement is not common, but when it does occur it often indicates important aspects of the interactive pattern. In this instance, the main character is Japanese (or Japanese American). His name and title are given for all to read. The American man, turned away from the camera, has no corresponding title. He is nameless, titleless, but nonetheless attentive to his Japanese companion. This forward-facing pattern together with the bright sunlight that illuminates the man's smiling face contrast with the off-center, back-to-the-camera Western man. Many additional details of the advertisement, if fully studied, support this interpretation. These include the potential for the reader to link the meaning of this advertisement with Japan's self-image as "the land of the rising sun," the contrast between the chairs in which the men sit, the upraised glass in the hand of one man, and so on. This advertisement also makes for an interesting comparison with the advertisement in Figure 3.12, where it is the Westerner who faces forward and the non-Westerner who is turned away from a frontal view.

FRIDAY

7月27日号(毎週金曜日発行)

昭和59年12月22日第三種郵便物認可 平成2年7月27日発行第7巻第30号 通巻第366号

編集人 森岩 弘 発行人 鈴木俊男 発売所 株式会社 講談社 〒112 東京都文京区音羽2—12—21 ☎03(945)1111(大代表) ☎03(943)2500(編集直通)

定価200円 (本体194円)

雑誌 22214—7/27 T4912221407208 NO.30 ©講談社 1990 凸版印刷 Printed in Japan

Figure 7.16

In addition to these aspects of the advertisement that support Japanese superiority in taste, status, and technology, the use of an American setting and an American man in the advertisement draws on some current conceptions of what America has to offer Japan. Perhaps the most significant of these are the openness and freedom of the American countryside along with the model presented here for relaxing and enjoying life.

Whichever of these or other meanings the reader associates with this advertisement, it is likely that they will support in some manner the contrast between Japan and America. In many ways this contrast will favor Japan. As America and Americans are utilized, they are decontextualized to significant degrees and romanticized. Openness, freedom, enjoyment—these sorts of issues that are predicated on images of America are most potent when they are juxtaposed with their opposites.

Another context in which Westerners appear in Japanese advertisements is as mannequins. This usage articulates the widely held aesthetic belief that Western clothes look better on Western models than on Japanese people. By contrast, Western companies rarely use Japanese or other Asian models in clothing advertisements. Western clothes are very common in Japan, but Japanese clothes are so rare in the West that there are no conventions about displaying them, no parallels to Japanese promotions for Western fashions. A more appropriate comparison would be to American advertisements for Japanese automobiles, which almost never show Japanese drivers. The imported cars are stripped of all Japanese cultural identity except for the association of high quality in the manufacturing process.

An advertisement for Gianni Versace (Figure 7.17) employs an unmistakably non-Japanese model to demonstrate the elegance of Italian men's fashions. The model is decontextualized. He appears against a pastel background, removed from all social and cultural context. He is merely a means of demonstrating the stylish clothes. He speaks no words that are represented to the viewer in writing. His face is almost expressionless, his eyes staring back at those who gaze upon him.

Similarly, the female model in Figure 7.18 is the mechanism for demonstrating Adam & Eve tableware. This highly stylized evocation contains this slogan down the left side of the page: "Adam & Eve exist inside of me." Except for a description of the Adam & Eve company as dealing in contemporary aesthetics, there are no words in this advertisement to explain who this woman is, what her life is like, or where she comes from. She is merely a prop. Whether the verbal reference is to Adam and Eve living in the tableware or in the woman or, as is most likely, in both, the reader must decide. The visual references suggest in a remote and removed manner the Western biblical origin myth. The reader may ponder how this woman is like Eve, whether the wrapped spherical object is an apple, and what the painter standing in the forest (garden?) on her hat is painting. Perhaps the viewer who knows a lot about the West will draw fully upon these signifiers.

What emerges for most Westerners when they first encounter such uses of Western models and cultural references in Japanese advertisements is an element of surprise. Why so many references to the West? What do these things mean to the Japanese—most of whom bear little physical resemblance to the Western models and for whom Adam and Eve and the American West are not connected very much with everyday life or cultural heritage? These are the kinds of questions that an encounter with the appropriated images and ideas evokes in those whose cultures are used in such a manner.

The strangeness of the representation of one's culture often deepens when some of the references are made more explicit. For example, the advertisement in Figure 7.19 draws upon the American heartland and a narrative about American life to sell mayonnaise. In American advertising such a technique to promote so mundane a product is unfamiliar. It is too remote, too distantly connected to the product. But beyond this, one wonders why this photograph and this story have been selected. Do they somehow represent Japanese ideas about America? If so, what are they? And why do they think these things?

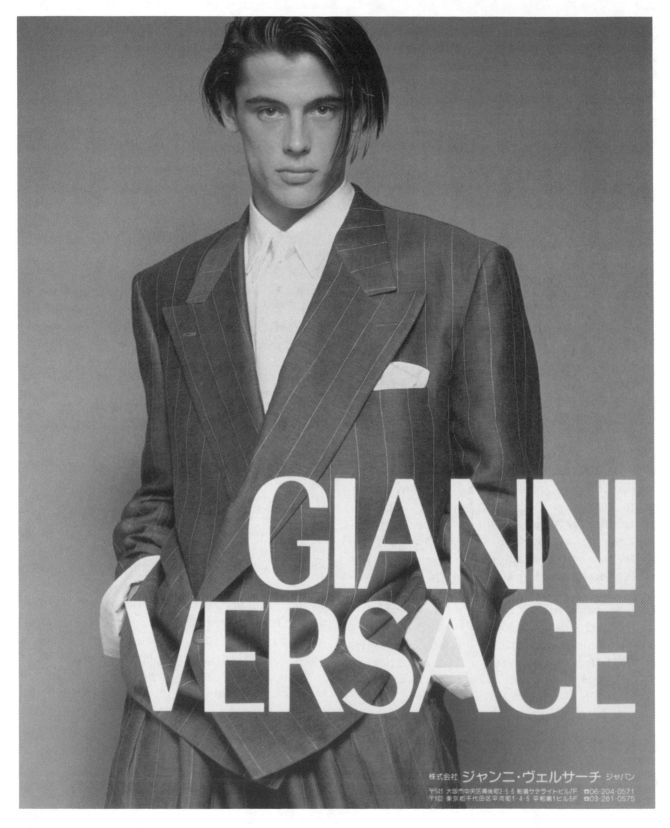

株式会社 ジャンニ・ヴェルサーチ ジャパン
〒541 大阪市中央区備後町2-5-6 船場サテライトビル7F ☎06-204-0571
〒102 東京都千代田区平河町1-4-5 平和第1ビル5F ☎03-261-0575

Figure 7.17

Figure 7.18

②

アメリカ大陸の秋は、最初に水の上に来る。

このあたりは、もう秋ね。とミシェールが言った。オハイオ川に近いみずうみで
僕たちはコマーシャルのための桟橋をさがしている。ミシェールは交換留学生で
日本で生活したこともあり、日本語も少し読める。それにタフだ。カーラジオで
ビートルズの曲がかかったとき、アメリカにはイーグルスがあるとつぶやいた。
だから、そんなに若くはない。ランチにしましょう。ターキーのサンドイッチ。
アイスボックスからマスタードとマヨネーズを出す。ガールフレンドは、新しい
人できた。ノーだ。だって、日本では恋の多くは夏はじまると言うでしょう。
それは広告のコピー。そして、秋に別れるのね。彼女はフリーウエイの入口の
スーパーマーケットで買ったリンゴをかじった。ケンタッキーのリンゴらしく
まだ固い。アメリカではね、恋は秋にはじまるの。ハイスクールの頃からね。

Figure 7.19

The caption above the photograph reads: "Fall on the American continent arrives first above the water." The narrative below it tells this story:

"It's already fall around here, huh," Michelle said. At a lake near the Ohio River, we are looking for a pier to shoot a commercial at. Michelle was an exchange student; she's lived in Japan and she can read a little Japanese. And she's tough. When a Beatles song came on the car radio, she said, "We have the Eagles in America." So she's not that young. Let's have lunch. Turkey sandwiches. We get the mustard and the mayonnaise out of the icebox. "Did you get a new girlfriend?" The answer is no. Well, in Japan, they say, people fall in love in the summer. That's only the copy of an ad. And they break up in the autumn, right? She had a bite of the apple that she had bought at a supermarket at the entrance to the freeway. Like an apple from Kentucky, it is still unripe. In America people fall in love in the fall. Beginning in high school, you know?

Interpreting what advertisements like this mean within the Japanese advertising tradition is a little like telling a joke and then having to explain its meaning. The listener may eventually comprehend, but the humor is lost. Figure 7.20 puts us as foreigners into this context. The headline in larger letters to the right of the picture reads, "I stocked up on three jokes that are bound to work." The smaller print further right says, "Tonight is special. The whiskey of choice is Crown Royal." The narrative around the picture of the two Western models runs:

Even when you're with somebody you're very compatible with, or even when you're trying really hard to pay attention, sometimes conversation can stop suddenly. Sometimes a pause can become really awkward. "Have I said something wrong?" "I messed up—" The nervous silence gradually begins to fill the room, spoiling the special time alone that the two of you were supposed to share. … It doesn't matter if you're experienced or not: this sudden moment is always a moment of fear. What saves such a moment is a sense of humor—a clever wit. (Not a vulgar one!) Unfortunately, though, this is not one of Japanese people's strong points. Both the teller and the listener of the joke are bad at what they're doing—and sometimes, somebody may even get mad. True, it's impossible to improve your sense of humor overnight. But when you have a big night ahead of you, you should stock up on a couple of new jokes. Even if you just have a few, if just one is successful, it will carry you through the awkward moment and make your conversation lively again. …

At this point the advertisement contains these three jokes:

Nobody is better than this. The best salesperson in the world is the young lady who sells her boyfriend the ring she is going to receive from him.
Now and then. "When I was young," said the father to his son, "I used to work twelve hours a day." "I see," said the son. "I envy your old days. These days if you take twelve hours to finish your job, you'll be fired at once."
Hobby. "I need some extra money for my hobby," said Bob. "Your hobby? This is the first time I've heard about your hobby," said Mike. "What's your hobby?" "Well, living, eating, and dressing."

These jokes are credited to a book entitled *Pocket Jokes*. The story continues:

Once your conversation has started to roll smoothly, you should choose a whiskey that won't interrupt its flow. The lightness of Crown Royal is best. It goes down smoothly and will never leave you tongue-tied. In addition, it has elegant depth. This Canadian whiskey is perfect for adult nights. Crown Royal: the Canadian whiskey dedicated to the king of England. Now, we dedicate it to adult men and women who want to spend meaningful nights together.

The interpretation of these jokes within the Japanese cultural context demands an understanding of the values placed in contemporary Japan on marketing abilities and dedication to work. Their understanding is enhanced by knowledge of gender differences in the workplace, the relations between men and their fathers, and the problems associated with finding time for enjoyment. There are some aspects of these jokes that are understand-

気の効いたジョークを3つほど仕入れた。

どんなに相性の良い相手といっしょでも、どんなに気を遣っていても。唐突に会話が冷えこんでしまうときがある。ふたりを包む空気がぎごちなくなるときがある。失言してしまったのだろうか、はずしてしまった…。哀しい沈黙が、じわじわと触手を伸ばしてきて、ふたりの素敵であるべき時間を蝕みはじめる。

そのままにしておくと、天使がどこからか飛んできて、わがもの顔にふたりの頭上を往き来し、台無しのまっ白い一夜をプレゼントしてくれるだろう。どんなに場数を踏んでいても、いきなりはじまる恐怖の一瞬。

これを救ってくれるのは、思わずクスッとさせるユーモア。なるほど、と感嘆させるウイット。(下品な笑いではない?)

ところが、残念ながらこのセンスは、日本人には不得手なもののひとつ。ジョークの送り手も、受け手も、どうもヘタで、なかには真剣に怒ってしまう無粋な人もいたりする。まあ、一朝一夕でユーモアのセンスを磨くのは苦しいとしても、大切な夜に臨むに際しては、新しいジョークを仕入れておくべきである。少なくとも、気の効いたジョークはたとえひとつでも、天使が通り過ぎるのをふせいでくれる。そして、ふたりの会話をスムーズにしてくれるはずである。

世界一のセールスマンは――ボーイフレンドに自分でもらう婚約指輪を売った娘である。右にでるものなし

for King and Queen
Crown Royal
希望小売価格7,500円 (消費税込み)
IMPORTED by KIRIN-SEAGRAM
(飲酒は20歳になってから)

今と昔
「わしが若い頃は」と父親が息子に言った。「一日十二時間働いたもんだ」
「なるほど」と息子が言った。「昔はよかったよ。今日び、一日の仕事をするのに十二時間もかかるやつはすぐにクビだもんね」

趣味
「趣味のために少し余分の金が必要なんだ」とボブが打ち明けた。
「趣味? 初耳だな」
「きみの趣味ってなんだい?」
「衣食住さ」

角川書店 植松 黎編・訳 ポケットジョークより

ふたりの会話が、スムーズにはずみだしたら、ウイスキーは、流れを邪魔しないものがいい。クラウン ローヤルのこの軽さがいい。のどをなめらかに滑り落ち、ことばを途切れさせない。そして、上品な深さ。このカナディアンウイスキーは、大人の夜にいちばんしっくりする。

イギリス国王に捧げられたカナディアンウイスキー クラウン ローヤル。夜を濃く過ごす大人の男と女に捧げます。

able outside the Japanese cultural context, but they are not—in a Western context—gems of cleverness.

The idealization of Western notions about beauty is another surprising aspect of Japanese advertising. Many advertisements for cigarettes, alcohol, and cosmetics contain Western models, some of whom may be contemporary celebrities like Madonna or classic ones like Audrey Hepburn. When these items are imported from the West, this connection is more readily understandable than when Western ideas of beauty are projected onto Japanese-made products, as for example in Figure 7.21 showing Whitest Essence from Shiseido, Japan's largest and most successful cosmetic company.

This adoration of Western ideals of beauty reaches an extreme form in the many contemporary advertisements for ways to make Japanese eyes look more Western. Some advertisements recommend cosmetic surgery to achieve the double-eyefold look. Others offer products that allow users to simulate this effect short of resorting to surgery. Figure 7.22 promotes a glue. It reads in part:

People who have unfolded eyelids can make them look like folded eyelids as long as they have the appropriate muscle. The Autoliner EX took this into account. Our product contains as a major ingredient a substance called moist resin, which we imported from West Germany, a country of advanced medicine. It is very safe and reliable. Our ultramodern technique works just like an eyeliner and keeps your eyelids folded—without hurting your muscles.

Figure 7.23, which promotes mascara, features a Western model whose eyes have the desirable double fold, unlike the nation of women who will see the advertisement.

One has merely to flip through the pages of current magazines to see further nuances in the use of Westerners in Japanese advertising. Increasingly, Westerners appear as cute and appealing. They are foreigners behind whose strangeness lies lovability. They do things Japanese would never do, but it is their misunderstanding of Japanese customs and language that makes them so appealing. In television commercials this often takes the form of Westerners' mispronouncing Japanese words or phrases. That they try but still get it wrong is what makes them cute. In Figure 7.24 the young man exhibits a degree of freedom and craziness that would be rare in Japan. But it is this that makes him appealing. The copy reads: "The Comfortable Party [in the sense of political party]. Even if I wear it every day, it's comfortable. Whoever wears it, it looks fashionable. BVD Comfort Underwear. Absorbency, durability, and comfort are all good. In addition, there are a lot of colors and patterns—"berrie goodo" [English, "very good"]. Well, c'mon men—start your collection!"

Finally, there are some uses of Westerners that can be described only as objectification. The caption of an advertisement promoting a yogurt drink (Figure 7.25) reads, "It's because I had a morning kiss that I am humming." The copy beneath says, "I kiss to become beautiful. Joa contains vitamins A, C, and other nutrients all of which are good for your health. We do research properly so our product is always lively. Let's have good kisses, shall we? Joa: 'goodo baransu' [English, "good balanced"] nutrition."

Looking at this advertisement from afar, one asks: Why does this Western girl appear in this particular advertisement? What do kissing and yogurt have to do with one another? Why is this girl turned into an object of some foreigner's sexuality? The more we study this advertisement, the less we understand from afar why an advertisement for a yogurt drink needs to use a young Western model talking about kissing. But this objectification of the West in Japanese advertising has its parallels in Western advertisements that portray foreign women as submissive, sensual, and willing to satisfy the tourist's every desire. The difference here is who is the active agent in the relationship and who is being objectified.

When we as an unexpected audience encounter Japanese advertisements for the first time, we are likely to react to them in various and complex ways. Most of all, we cannot but find a discrepancy between how we are represented in these advertisements and what we think about ourselves. Although we recognize the aspects of our culture that

もうシミ、ソバカスに悩まない。

発売4か月で何と一〇〇万個も売れたという
話題の美容液が資生堂〝ホワイテス　エッセンス〟。

シミ、ソバカスの回復に高い効果を表す
その秘密は、アルブチンという成分。

資生堂が8年の歳月をかけて研究したという、
シミ、ソバカスに画期的なパワーを発揮する
アルブチンって、一体何!?

お問い合わせ先・SHISEIDO㈱ 03-572-5111

Figure 7.21

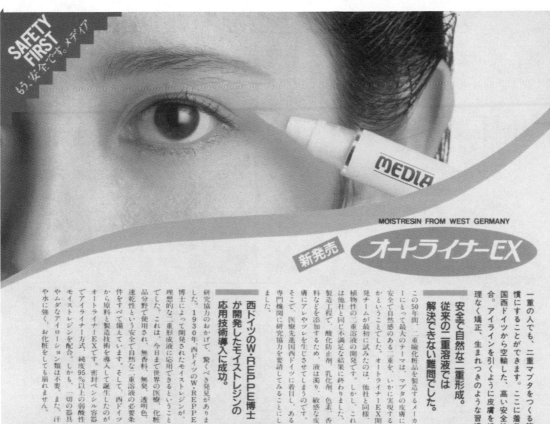

Figure 7.22

Figure 7.23

Figure 7.24

• 191

はな歌がでてしまうのは、
モーニング・キッスを
したからです。

キレイになるため、キスをする。
ジョアには、おなかの健康に良い
乳酸桿菌（L.カゼイ・シロタ株）と、
消化吸収されやすい
ビタミンA・Cも含まれ、
しっかり科学しています。
だから、いつも生き生き。
おいしい口づけ、いたしましょう。

栄養のグッドバランス
ジョア

(株)ヤクルト本社 〒105 東京都港区東新橋1-1-19 Tel 03(5719)8960
お客さま相談センターフリーダイヤル 0120-11-8960

are selected for use in the Japanese advertisements, the emphasis given to them is unusual. But like stereotypes in other contexts, these have bases in reality. It is their exaggeration we are likely to reject. Additionally, when we find ourselves objectified, even to the point of being the unwanted objects of someone else's sexual fantasies, we are almost certainly made uncomfortable by such a situation, and our reactions may be even stronger. But as we react to such representations of America and the West, we must ask ourselves, Is this not what we have done in our advertisements to peoples and cultures who are defined as *other?*

Someone Else's Dream

Since 1986 about a dozen books on American advertising in the 1950s and 1960s, lavishly illustrated with reprints of advertisements, have appeared in Japanese bookstores. Their English-language titles, such as *American Romance, American Memory, The '60s: America Portrayed Through Advertisements,* provide a key to their contents, but they do not explain why Japanese readers might find such items from the past interesting.

Yasutoshi Ikuta's English-language foreword to *American Romance* is more helpful:

When you clean your room for the first time in many days, you happen to find one old teen-age girl's magazine. While you read page by page, unconsciously you must leave your work aside and your mind goes back and drifts into memories of your childhood.

Everyone must have such experience. Old magazines, old newspapers and your old diary. … they are always "carefree" but high performance time-machines.

Full-color illustrations collected in this book are the advertisements appearing in American text and picture weeklies of the '50s.

About 80 illustrations were severely chosen to suit the title of this book, out of over 20 thousand advertising clippings which had been kept carefully for more than 30 years, and they are reproduced by the best high-tech printing and plate making techniques.

Each page is so fantastic and provoking nostalgia.

Because the '50s when these advertisements appeared was the last period in which men were man-like and ladies were ladylike. …

Please look at them calmly, then before you notice, you must go into the dreaming world of the '50s.

Let's go on a trip to the good old days of America, using the time-machine called old magazine advertisements.

All aboard! Now, it's leaving in a moment!

Figures 7.26 through 7.29 appear in Ikuta's books. He provides only general commentary rather than interpreting individual advertisements. Consequently, an American who happens upon these books in a Tokyo bookstore may browse through them and wonder just what it is that Japanese readers find interesting in them. It certainly cannot be the technology of the Pontiac Catalina in Figure 7.26 that is so impressive; is it perhaps the uncrowded highway and the unhurried lives of the people in the car? Is it the large, well-lit house in the background? Or is it the woman's pleasure at having the door opened for her by the man?

Similarly, what does Figure 7.27 suggest to its Japanese audience? Is the fascination here with the vacation? Knowing how to have a good time? Relaxing in a family context? The spaciousness of the countryside? As an unintended audience for these books, an American reader cannot easily know how another accidental audience interprets them. The advertisements reprinted in Ikuta's books no longer have their function of promoting products. They only serve in this secondary context to relay information about the values and life-styles of the periods in American history they depict.

When we study Figure 7.28, we wonder what it is about the beach scene that is so interesting. Americans who lived through the 1950s and the 1960s know that the collection of friends in the picture was also a dream world at home. This set of people is all white, securely paired up in male-female couples, and living the good life. When it appeared in

The Magnificent **STAR CHIEF**
WRAPS UP EVERYTHING !

*Customized Luxury and Sports Car Performance
put this Strato-Streak Beauty in a Class by Itself!*

Every ride in this gleaming masterpiece is a sparkling special occasion!

You're surrounded by the soft glow of exclusive Catalina colors translated in shimmering nylon, supple, hand-rubbed leather and rich carpeting. You command America's newest and most thrilling performance team— the breath-taking power of the mighty Strato-Streak V-8, the hair-trigger quick, yet creamy-smooth response of Strato-Flight Hydra-Matic*.

In the way it looks and the way it goes, there's no match for this regal Catalina—*at any price!* A brief inspection and short demonstration drive will prove it. Come in and see. **An extra-cost option.*

SEE YOUR PONTIAC DEALER

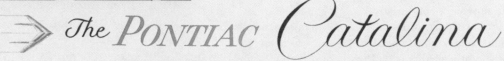

The PONTIAC *Catalina*

The new 1954 Chevrolet Delray Coupe. With three great series Chevrolet offers the most beautiful choice of models in its field.

Four good reasons why new Chevrolet families are "having a wonderful time"...

That family up there has everything it takes to enjoy a wonderful vacation—a fine place to go and a fine new Chevrolet to get them there.

In fact, no other car fits so beautifully into all your family activities all the year 'round.

FIRST OF ALL, there's a lot of pride and pleasure for you in Chevrolet's lasting good looks. It's the only low-priced car, with Body by Fisher. And *that*, you know, means smarter styling outside and in, and more solid quality through and through. You'll see it in the finer workmanship and materials, the greater comforts and conveniences.

THEN THAT FINE AND THRIFTY Chevrolet performance is always a special pleasure. Chevrolet's high-compression power—highest of any leading low-priced car —brings smoother, quicker response and important

gasoline savings, too. Here's one car that's really easy to handle and park on shopping trips, and that gives you solid and steady big-car comfort on vacation trips.

AND BEST OF ALL, MAYBE, is the eager, quiet, uncomplaining way your Chevrolet keeps on going wherever and whenever you want to go. You can count on it to start quickly and run smoothly night or day, fair weather or foul. You won't find another car with such a great name for serving its owners reliably and economically over a long, long life span.

FOURTH BUT NOT LEAST, we'll be glad to show you how beautifully a new Chevrolet will fit your budget, too. For Chevrolet is priced below all other lines of cars.

See Your Chevrolet Dealer

BRIGHT NEW IDEA IN INTERIORS! The interior of the new Chevrolet Delray Club Coupe is all vinyl, in colors that harmonize with the exterior finish. It's as practical as it is beautiful, for the vinyl is easily washable and amazingly resistant to scuffing and wear.

YEAR AFTER YEAR MORE PEOPLE BUY CHEVROLETS THAN ANY OTHER CAR!

Figure 7.27

• 195

Figure 7.28

"Here's the roomy G-E Refrigerator my family won't outgrow!"

Figure 7.29   •   197

1956, this was for most Americans more a fantasy than a close reflection of their lives.

And what does it mean to a Japanese audience in the 1990s to look into the airbrushed world of the early 1950s as depicted in Figure 7.29? Now that Japan has equal or superior technology for domestic appliances, of what significance are the large American refrigerator and the storybook family who surround it?

Thus far, only one of Yasutoshi Ikuta's books has been published in the United States. He maintains that he has no plans to publish these books in America for an American audience. Rather, his books are directed to a reading public that wants to imagine America as its opposite. These books construct a Japanese fantasy about America and its past—a world of beautiful people, large cars, and opulent life-styles. The reprinted advertisements have no necessary connection to what America is like today or even, for that matter, what it ever was. These books are Japanese dreams of America that parallel American dreams about Japan.

Bibliographic Notes

The images Japan and the West developed of one another are described by Endymion Wilkinson in his book *Japan Versus the West: Image and Reality* (London: Penguin, 1990). The incorporation and absorption of American ideas and consumer goods into Japanese culture is the subject of the essays in *Re-made in Japan: Everyday Life and Consumer Taste in a Changing Society*, edited by Joseph J. Tobin (New Haven: Yale University Press, 1992).

George Fields's books on Japanese marketing include analyses of Japanese advertising, including the use of foreigners in modern Japanese advertising. Especially useful are his *From Bonsai to Levi's: When West Meets East, an Insider's Account of How the Japanese Live* (New York: Macmillan, 1983), *The Japanese Market Culture* (Tokyo: Japan Times, 1989), and *Gucci on the Ginza: Japan's New Consumer Generation* (Tokyo: Kodansha, 1989). Anthropologist Millie R. Creighton has assessed "Images of Foreigners in Japanese Advertising" in the 1992 proceedings of the Japan Studies Association of Canada (forthcoming).

Yasutoshi Ikuta's books on American advertising include *American Romance: The World of Advertising Art* (1988), *American Memory: The World of Advertising Art* (Tokyo: Heibonsha, 1988), *The '60s: America Portrayed Through Advertisements* (Tokyo: Graphic-sha, 1989), *American Car Graffiti, 1902–1936* (Tokyo: Jitsugyo No Nihonsha, 1986), and *'50s American Magazine Ads* (Tokyo: Graphic-sha, 1987).

Readers may wish to consult one or more of the many books published in the United States and Europe on Japanese business. Some of these give advice on how to conduct business with the Japanese, for example, Neil Chesanow, *The World-Class Executive: How to Do Business Like a Pro Around the World* (New York: Rawson Associates, 1985). Others are more general analyses of how Japan came to be so significant an economic power in the modern world and attempt to assess future trends, for example, Bill Emmott, *The Sun Also Sets* (New York: Times Books, 1989).

The Future

WHAT OF THE FUTURE? Are there signs of fundamental change in the depictions of ourselves and others that constitute the discourse of advertising? Will the imbalances of power continue to be depicted in the secondary messages of advertisements whose surfaces only purport to be about goods and services? Contemporary efforts to predict the future, like alchemy and astrology in other ages, are at best inexact. Even worse, many times they are wrong. Nonetheless, there are some indications of what trends we may expect in the next decade and beyond.

The globalization of markets is one of the most salient issues for business. The world has moved beyond local and regional markets. Even export to other countries of goods produced at home is no longer the latest business innovation. Manufacturing, once confined to the industrialized nations of Europe and America, has now shifted to many Third World nations, where labor and materials can be obtained more inexpensively than in the developed nations. Assembly lines now extend across national borders.

Global commodities and services have emerged in the late twentieth century. McDonald's, now in countless countries around the world, offers essentially the same hamburgers everywhere. Marlboro cigarettes are for sale in small hamlets the world over as well as in Singapore, Nairobi, and Buenos Aires. International commerce seems to know no borders and to be unstopped by linguistic or cultural differences. Whether it takes the form of Coke, Pepsi, or some other soft drink, the experience of refreshment in a bottle is no longer strange to people of any culture.

The globalization of goods and services raises anew the issue of the universality of human wants and aspirations. The question emerges whether universal symbols and representations can be used in advertising around the globe or whether it will be necessary to duplicate efforts to find local selling messages to promote global products.

Coca-Cola's experience is instructive in this regard. Lying behind its advertising is a complex structure for producing advertising messages that contain universal themes but are sensitive to local cultural differences. Working out of the New York office of McCann-Erickson, a team of writers and producers create television commercials and print advertisements that can be used in many different countries. Some important techniques facilitate this process. The commercials almost never include any person speaking on camera. By relying on musical or voice-over soundtracks, the advertisers make substitutions of language a relatively easy matter. Because the actors look neither too Scandinavian nor too Mediterranean, they can be imagined to be nationals of many different countries whose populations have European heritage. By shooting commercials in Australia, Brazil, Italy, England, and a host of other countries, the creative team comes to understand intuitively the place of Coca-Cola in global culture. They sense the universal elements and have a feel for what is too local or too specific to be included in commercial intended to be shown across the world.

Behind this effort is a philosophy of thinking globally and acting locally. Marcio Moriera, international creative director for McCann-Erickson, explains that representations that may on the surface appear different can have underlying common ideas. For example, Sprite (a noncola soft drink made by the Coca-Cola company) is often linked to beach scenes and water imagery. The intent is to convey ideas of wetness and young people having fun and to connect these notions to Sprite. This is the idea behind the global conceptualization of the advertising for this brand. But there are some problems that must be taken into account. Differences between Brazilian and Arab sensitivities to scantily clad men and women playing on a beach require shooting different versions of the commercial so that each version will fit local cultural values. Some nations like Korea and Australia require that the principal actors in television commercials be nationals. These laws mean that commercials produced for a world market may need to be reshot by some regional offices. In South Africa Sprite commercials directed to the indigenous market include neither beach scenes nor water imagery. Swimming is uncommon, and beaches have traditionally been a playground for whites, but research showed that roller-skating had much the same meaning. The local execution of the global idea of youth, fun, and Sprite, then, is realized in a commercial that, on the surface, does not look much like the more common beach scenes. A superficial examination of advertisements may mislead; behind apparent differences may indeed lie more universal themes.

Thus global markets have equivalents in generic consumers. The consumer of a hamburger or a Coke may look different in Japan, Africa, and Latin America, but the equation of product and benefit for the consumer may in fact be a rather common message. The formula may be expressed in somewhat different guises, but the message can be the same. Contemporary advertising practitioners know this, and they make their very best attempts to find a single effective message. It is both an economy of scale and a minimization of unnecessarily duplicated effort.

Perhaps one of the consequences of the globalization of markets, the increase in the availability of the same goods and services around the world, and the emergence of generic consumers who are portrayed as sharing common desires will be a decrease in the otherness of foreigners. A Japanese girl drinking a Coke has a lot in common with a French or Brazilian girl drinking a Coke. What consumers in these countries and in others can see in such advertisements are the things they share with other people, not the things that separate them and make them different. But in speculating about what more advertisements of this sort might mean, we should not assume too quickly that otherness will disappear. Rather, what is significant is that there is for the first time in the representation of social patterns and cultural values an effort to find the "ideas that travel" and the images that communicate across linguistically and culturally distinctive regions of the world. As this becomes more common, the discourse of advertising will resonate around shared aspirations, life-styles, and values.

The Return of Individually Tailored Messages

The time has long passed when buying and selling was an unmediated interpersonal activity that took place in an open-air market or even a department store. Prepackaged vegetables in supermarkets and merchandise bought through catalogs have made such activities very old-fashioned. The contemporary marketplace is less and less a physical location than an abstraction. Twentieth-century media innovations have changed buying and selling. Indeed, we are now accustomed—and often jaundiced in our reactions—to commercials that offer us mail-order bargains in the middle of the night. All we need do, we are instructed, is to call a toll-free number where operators stand by around the clock to take our orders. We never see these people who answer the telephone, and we have learned not to ask them questions about the goods or services offered in the television commercials. They take orders; they do not demonstrate products.

These homogeneous messages may be on the wane. More narrowly focused messages that are better fitted to our consuming profiles are on the rise. Behind this lies increasingly sophisticated market research on which the messages may be based. When advertisers claim to reflect society, they often have reference to the research that has been conducted to determine what potential consumers think and may be willing to purchase. By taking this information and using it in constructing the messages about the benefits of goods and services to consumers, the messages better articulate with the recipients.

The volume of this type of research is astounding. However, market research, unlike academic social science research, is usually proprietary. It amounts to a private sociology and psychology of the consumer society that will never be available beyond very narrow limits. Once collected and used for intended purpose, such information is often not saved. Profiles of consumers become dated quickly and cease to have relevance to business decisions. And because neither the advertising agencies nor the companies they represent are historical archives, most research reports are destroyed. In addition to a general lack of interest in history, businesses sometimes find that destroying documents may have legal advantages later. However, some examples of this research are made public from time to time.

An indication of the information that might be used in this manner was discussed in a May 13, 1988, *Wall Street Journal* article on consumer psychology. The article reported in considerable detail research conducted by McCann-Erickson for a potential client who manufactures and sells bug spray. The company was considering making insect-killing plastic strips that could be put in cabinets and closets and would work instead of the smellier and messier sprays. The agency's research included psychological profiles of heavy users of the product. This research showed these consumers to be working women in their middle years living in the southern United States. The research included focus-group discussions with bug spray users as well as studies of psychological profiles, including fears and fantasies about bugs. The researchers found that the women talked about the bugs as male gendered and had little interest in strips of plastic that the manufacturer proposed to offer for sale. The women, especially in their dreams and fantasies, talked about fears of being attacked by bugs and wanting to kill them directly

with the bug spray rather than allowing the bugs to sneak around or hide in cabinets. Because McCann-Erickson did not get the account, this research was not treated as proprietary but was given as an example to a newspaper reporter inquiring about the nature of current market research. Yet we can extrapolate from it some understanding of the depth of knowledge about consumers that lies behind advertising messages. Advertisements do reflect social patterns and cultural values in significant ways. The accuracy of this reflection is due in part to the vast amount of research conducted about these patterns and values. The knowledge about consumers that advertisers have allows for a better articulation of advertising messages with consumer profiles.

Another factor associated with a repersonalization of messages is the nature of the mass media themselves. Cable television, broadcasts by satellite, and videocassettes changed the nature of the most pervasive mass medium. According to trade journal reports, it is now technically possible to send different commercial messages into different households. This would mean that a family having a dog could receive a dog food commercial whereas their neighbors with a cat could receive a cat food commercial. The superfluous and irrelevant messages could be weeded out. To set this technology in place, however, would require detailed knowledge about the social (and psychological) profiles and consumption patterns of households. Only concerns about the invasion of privacy have limited the development of such personalized messages. But the issue here is not a technical one. Advertisers are ready to direct more-tailored messages to consumers, and we may well see these in the coming years.

There are already some ways in which this process is at work. In *The Clustering of America* (1988), Michael J. Weiss describes how zip codes alone can tell marketers a great deal about the people living in different regions of the United States. By dividing the 250,000 neighborhoods into forty-three patterns, direct-mail marketers can select and target those zip codes that are most likely to yield potential consumers. Similarly, psychological profiles of consumers resulted in the values and life-styles system (VALS) that became widely used in the 1980s. In analogy to the demographic profiling of consumers, VALS proposed "psychographics" of the American population. Advertisements based on this system attempted to target specifically those individuals whose values and life-styles correspond most directly to the goods or services promoted.

The most innovative personalization of messages has begun to occur in those advertisements that invite audience collaboration. Perfume and fashion advertising uses this technique heavily. Guess jeans and Calvin Klein in particular rely on visual images that do not tell a complete story. Rather, they invite the audience to take the images offered in the advertisements and to do with them as they will. Even automobile advertising has begun to experiment with this technique. But what is most critical about this advertising is the personalization of the message.

These techniques draw heavily on the Japanese advertising tradition where images are used to evoke feelings and moods. Potential consumers who like the evocations may in turn become actual consumers. Whether this will work in a more matter-of-fact America remains to be seen. However, its presence and potential increase is further indication of the degree to which mass messages are giving way to more personal ones, even if they are mediated in complex ways through the media in which they are presented.

A New Economic Order

As these changes occur in messages and media, important alterations of the economic order within society are also taking place. In particular, the late twentieth century is characterized by a greatly increased number of people who have large amounts of discretionary income to spend on consumer goods and services. Thus the manufacturing of goods and the offering of services to the affluent sector of the population is a major concern among businesspeople.

Paralleling this emergent class of newly affluent Americans are others who are not so well-off. These people must make more cautious economic decisions. They are more concerned about working within family budgets than with the management of discretionary income. In addition to these less affluent Americans are the homeless poor. Although the discourse of advertising has little to say to these people directly, they nonetheless see the images of the good life and compare their own failure to the models held up within the advertisements.

What all this means is that an economically based class system is replacing the American myth of the great middle class. No longer is it fashionable to maintain that one is middle class like everyone else. Rather, distinctions among people based on patterns of consumption are an important part of current social order. Nowhere is this better exemplified than in airline travel, where three classes of service are offered. Similarly, hotel chains and restaurants cater either to the budget-minded or to business travelers or to luxury travelers. The ends of the socioeconomic continuum are moving further apart. Sears, once the mainstay of middle-class standards, is being replaced by Wal-Mart economy and by upscale boutique shopping. The same individuals may even frequent both types of stores on different occasions. A brand like French's on the mustard jar has been replaced in many kitchens by Grey Poupon and imported mustards or by cost-cutter, no-name brands. In the new scheme of things, we are what we consume.

The Management of Minds

At Duke University courses on film, media, and advertising became popular choices of undergraduates in the 1980s and 1990s. These interests have emerged at other colleges and universities as well. What accounts for the popularity of such concerns? Some answers emerge by comparing the "me generation" of the 1980s with preceding ones. For example, in the 1960s the end of colonialism and development was a major concern in the social sciences. Civil rights at home and political independence for former colonies in Africa and Asia raised questions about a reordering of social relations as the distribution of power changed. Trendy courses focused on the impact of these changes on society.

In the 1970s the oil crisis and the cold reality of the economic dependency of poorer nations on richer ones dampened enthusiasm about the new social order that had emerged in the 1960s. It quickly became apparent that the economic hardships of African Americans were not going to change overnight. In colleges and universities social theory focused on dependency and attempted to assess realistically why the old order was not likely to be transformed quickly.

The 1980s saw the emergence of yuppies and other self-indulgent groups. Long hair and political activism were replaced by concerns about strategies for success. Professors complained that students were too pre-professional in their interests and focused too heavily on themselves and their own interests. Altruism had little place on the college campus, save occasional protests or demonstrations for South African divestment or women's rights. In the midst of all this emerged the interest in the media and a concern with advertising.

At Duke an undergraduate class on advertising and society became one of the most popular courses in the 1980s. More conventional defenders of a classical curriculum saw this as the eventual outcome of the television generation's going to college. Accustomed to watching television all their lives, the critics could say, these students gravitated to classes where they could see films or watch videos. But there is another side to all this as well. It has to do with the recognition among these very students that television and advertising are fundamental parts of their lives. They grew up with the Muppets, Big Bird, and Miss Piggy. They cried when Mr. Hooper died. It seemed only sensible that they turn some of their interests to things more directly a part of their lives than pondering Heathcliff's wanderings on English moors or Caesar's battlefield strategies. In electing media studies, they were not denying a place for Shakespeare among their courses. Rather, they sought a curriculum that was broad enough to encompass all their experiences.

Having taught this course for more than a decade and having listened to hundreds of students speak and write about their ideas, I have come to believe that one of the deepest motives for studying the media is a fundamental desire to understand how our lives are shaped by the media. Curiosity about advertising is concern about the management of our lives and our value systems. The captains of consciousness who emerged in the late nineteenth century are very much at work. In the postindustrial society, they continue to be in the business of producing consumers by managing their ideas and beliefs. It is a concern with who these people are and why they do what they do that lies at the heart of students' current interest in advertising and the mass media. They are asking, as did generations of students before them, who is in charge and how they manage their power over others. The liberal arts study of advertising is ultimately very much about these questions.

What we find when we look into the relation between advertising and society is a value system depicted in the secondary messages of advertisements that is driven by the economy. Ultimately, the reasons why particular depictions are used in advertisements is that they work better. In advertising working better means that such depictions are better remembered and are more convincing messages. Thus certain portrayals of people and their relations with others are used because they are most effective in communicating the selling message. That the secondary messages are also communicated in advertisements and give people ideas about themselves, other people, and social relations are generally considered by advertisers to be incidental to the main business of advertising.

Authority, Domination, and Subordination

One of the readings that I have consistently assigned in the course on advertising and society is Stanley Milgram's *Obedience to Authority* (1974).

When they look through the books assigned for the course, many students initially think that the book list contains a mistake. All the other readings are about advertising or media; this one is about a set of psychology experiments in which people are required to administer an electric shock to another participant each time that person gives an incorrect answer to a question. The second participant does not actually receive a shock, but the experimental subject does not know this. The experimenter insists that the subject continue to shock the fellow participant and to increase the voltage over the course of the experiment. This demand is made despite the protestations of the second participant about the pain being inflicted by the shocks.

I use this book to direct attention to the matter of how people respond to authorities in their lives. (Milgram wrote the book as a part of his effort to understand how it was possible that Nazis had complied with the orders to inflict harm on other people.) The book occasions a discussion of the degree to which advertising and the mass media are authorities in our lives and whether we respond mindlessly to them, at times perhaps against our better interests. Initial resistance to comparing responses to advertising, which is about aspirations, to compliance with demands to commit wartime atrocities gives way to a consideration of the degree to which we acquiesce and why we so seldom complain to those who seek to manage our values and lives.

At this point I always ask for a show of hands of those who have written letters of complaint about advertisements. Only a very few hands go up. I relate a couple of personal experiences with my own letters of complaint (of which I also have only written a few). I tell about the time in graduate school when I was writing my dissertation and was too busy to cook for myself or go out for food. While opening a can of soup, I noticed the claim on the label that explained what a wonderful woman my family would think I was when I served them this soup. Perhaps my letter of outrage to the soup company was mostly a device to procrastinate. Whatever its real motive, the response interested me a great deal. The public relations officer wrote politely to explain that the claim was made because

their market research showed most of their customers were in fact women. She apologized for having offended me. But most importantly, she informed me that I was the only person to have made this complaint!

Another example I use is a letter that I wrote to Eastern Airlines following a flight from North Carolina to Chicago. We had a very loquacious pilot on this particular flight. I was en route to California to make a presentation. I was hoping to put the finishing touches on it while I was on the plane. His constant announcements about geography and weather were annoying. When we flew over Indiana, he told us that he was a native of that state and asked whether we knew that Hoagie Carmichael was also from Indiana. He proceeded to sing "Stardust." Some of the other passengers also seemed annoyed. One kept saying, "Who is this guy?" Following my return home, I wrote Frank Borman, who was then president of the company. A few weeks later, the pilot himself telephoned to apologize. He seemed genuinely surprised that I or anyone else was annoyed. Then he echoed a familiar refrain, "I had no idea. I thought everybody liked my comments. Nobody ever complained before."

Once when discussing this issue of consumer complaints with a group of adults who came to hear me talk about advertising, one member of the audience told me about how she had in fact written a letter complaining about a brochure that had been published by a local marketing concern. On its cover, she said, was a picture of an utterly helpless woman who looked as if she were handicapped. The woman was struggling in the grass to make her way to the house at some distance on a hilltop. She said that she had written the company to complain that their illustration on the brochure seemed insensitive to the plight of handicapped people and that she had not liked the illustration they had chosen. She also told them that she saw no relevance of the illustration to the items they had for sale.

In due course she received a letter from the company expressing their concern that they had offended her and possibly others. They maintained that it had not been their intention to do so. The writer pointed out that the illustration was a parody of Andrew Wyeth's *Christina's World* and that possibly had she known this, she would not have been offended. This woman's story pointed out the importance of remembering that advertisements mean what the audience thinks they mean. She had not understood the reference to Wyeth, and she had taken offense. In this instance her own authorship overrode the intentions of the graphic designer.

Each of these accounts merely illustrates the general point that consumers do relatively little complaining about what they find offensive in the secondary messages in the discourse of advertising. Those who prepare and disseminate the messages often interpret this silence as agreement. When consumers speak up—as they did about the symbols used by Procter and Gamble as trademarks—the advertisers and their clients take a different tack. Such complaints, they argue, amount to attempts to censor. Either way, what the message makers and sponsors are arguing is that they, not the consumers, should have the right to determine what is appropriate to include. Only when they determine that consumers may act on the basis of their convictions in the form of boycotting advertised products do changes get made. Companies are reluctant to offend potential consumers. They seek secondary messages that will work in the sense of being convincing and yet that will not offend and result in a boycott. These economic considerations drive the value system out of which the secondary messages of advertisements are constructed. Consumer complaints threaten the monopoly on the management of meaning that the producers of cultural ideas feel is rightly theirs. At issue is the determination of one's ideas of self, of society, and of others.

The Socialization of Consumers

The value system contained in the discourse of advertising—that is, both the first messages about what to consume and the second messages about how to live one's life—is taught from our earliest years. By its presence in our lives, sponsored television teaches some of the most important lessons that American children learn. Saturday morning commercials offer gender patterning: boys playing with fast cars and action toys, girls playing with dolls and domestic replicas. Concerned parental groups such as Action for Children's Television (ACT) publish literature to encourage greater involvement of parents in the content of television directed to children. They have focused on such issues as the quality of programming, violence, and nutrition. These are grand issues, and the obstacles in the way of change are significant.

Some other issues that might also be deemed worthy have not yet received much attention. In particular, the reasoning process taught by commercials deserves consideration. These advertisements amount to syllogisms that work like propositions, viewers being given information and then asked to draw conclusions. Stripped to their skeletal frameworks, most commercials have somewhat faulty logic that encourages forming conclusions without all the information that might be relevant. In deciding which breakfast cereal to buy, decisions made on the basis of such reasoning processes may not have very important social consequences. However, when this type of thinking, which is so deeply ingrained beginning in early childhood, is applied elsewhere—as, for example, in presidential elections—the consequences are more significant. Among the other things that massive exposure to television and commercials does is to teach children ways of making decisions. In addition, the models that appear on television also teach the very important lesson that children, too, are what they consume.

The Advertisers' Perspective

The response of advertising agencies and their client companies to such matters as consumer complaints and the effects of advertisements on children show us a great deal about their ideology of the proper distribution of power in society. Their responses also show that within American society there is no serious criticism of the discourse of advertising. Rather, criticism is restricted to academic ruminations, occasional rude books or other attacks on advertising, and a relatively low frequency of letters from consumers.

When they do respond to the content of the criticism, the advertisers justify their position by maintaining that their job is to put their sponsors' products in the best possible light. It is not the business of advertising, they say, to point out what is wrong with a promoted item. "Consumers vote with their pocketbooks" and "You can't sell a bad product twice" are standard defenses of the status quo in contemporary advertising.

On matters like sexism, racism, or the representation of foreigners, advertisers insist that they are only reflecting society. It is society that is sexist or racist. They claim to represent people and society as they are. What they resist is any acceptance of responsibility for the maintenance of such ideas by repeating them. They deny the generative role of advertising at the same time they claim that advertisements encourage people to buy and use new products or to switch brands of old ones.

It is also important to understand the way in which the discourse of advertising operates with regard to the particular people who articulate it. The active career of any person—a copywriter, an artist, or an account executive—is perhaps only forty years or so. Advertising is larger than this. It preexisted their involvement in it. Presumably it will exist after they have left an active career. Thus individuals who practice the craft of advertising enter the discourse, contribute to it, but often disclaim any real responsibility for what it said before or may say after they are involved in its production. Moreover, except for the very few who rise to the top creative and management positions, they also typically express little belief that they have much control over the processes of cultural production that make up the business of advertising. When we view the advertising world in this manner, we come to understand that individual practitioners are in the business of denying much responsibility for their

activities. When thousands of people maintain that ethical matters are someone else's concern, it sometimes happens (as in the case of Milgram's experiments) that individuals act without much sense of personal responsibility for their actions.

Possibilities for Change

When we understand advertising to operate without much effective control, we come to appreciate some of its further social consequences. Much like pornography, when viewed repeatedly, the discourse of advertising reiterates themes to which we ultimately become desensitized. This is what has happened with regard to the representation of foreigners in American advertising. We have become accustomed to the portrayal of ourselves as powerful and of others as powerless. The ideology of dominance and subordination becomes familiar. We even expect such ideas in other advertisements because we have seen them in the past. We become used to the images, the social relations, and the inequalities of power that make up the discourse of advertising. It is true in many ways that this discourse reflects social practices and cultural values already present, but it is simultaneously true that it recreates them in the process of depicting them. It becomes impossible to say which comes first: the culture or the ad.

Bibliographic Notes

The ideas in this chapter were collected from a variety of sources, including newspapers, trade journals, and popular books and magazines. There are few academic treatments of these issues. For further materials on these topics, I recommend a critical reading of such sources.

I published an interview with Marcio Moriera entitled "The Airbrushing of Culture," in *Public Culture* 2, 1, 1989. In it he speaks at great length about his understandings of trends in contemporary global advertising.

Differences in the attitudes and behaviors of people of different social classes is a bread-and-butter issue for the discipline of sociology. One of the most influential recent books on this topic is Pierre Bordieu's *Distinction: A So-*

cial Critique of the Judgement of Taste, trans. Richard Nice (Cambridge: Harvard University Press, 1984).

Since 1980 or so, Harvard Business School professor Theodore Levitt has published essays in the *Harvard Business Review* that deal with the globalization of markets. Some of his earlier essays were collected together in *The Marketing Imagination* (New York: Free Press, 1983). Readers interested in the emergence of modern advertising will find Stuart Ewen's *Captains of Consciousness: Advertising and the Social Roots of the Consumer Culture* (New York: McGraw-Hill, 1976) helpful.

References

Alsop, Ronald. 1988. "Advertisers Put Consumers on the Couch: Research Probes Emotional Ties to Products." *Wall Street Journal,* May 13, 21.

Boorstin, Daniel. 1973. "From Traveler to Tourist: The Lost Art of Travel," in his *The Image: A Guide to Pseudo-events in America.* New York: Atheneum.

Bourke-White, Margaret. Unpublished address delivered to a meeting of the creative staff of the J. Walter Thompson Company, New York, New York, on February 1, 1933. Original in J. Walter Thompson Company Archives, Special Collections Department, Perkins Library, Duke University, Durham, North Carolina.

Dennis, Lisl. 1979. *How to Take Better Travel Photos.* Tucson, Ariz.: Fisher.

Goldman, Robert. 1992. *Reading Ads Socially.* New York: Routledge.

Grosvenor, Gilbert. 1957. *The National Geographic Society and Its Magazine.* Washington, D.C.: National Geographic Society.

Ikuta, Yasutoshi. 1988. *American Romance: The World of Advertising Art.* Tokyo: Heibonsha.

Marchand, Roland. 1985. *Advertising the American Dream: Making Way for Modernity, 1920–1940.* Berkeley: University of California Press.

Milgram, Stanley. 1974. *Obedience to Authority.* New York: Harper & Row.

O'Rourke, Dennis. 1987. *Cannibal Tours.* Los Angeles: Direct Cinema Limited. Videotape.

Said, Edward. 1978. *Orientalism.* New York: Pantheon.

Weiss, Michael J. 1988. *The Clustering of America.* New York: Harper & Row.

Williams, Raymond. 1980. "Advertising: The Magic System," in his *Problems in Materialism and Culture.* London: Verso.

Williamson, Judith. 1978. *Decoding Advertisements: Ideology and Meaning in Advertising.* London: Marion Boyars.

About the Book and Author

IF, THROUGH THE YEARS, American advertising has offered a clean and simple approach to getting out the word on new products or services, it has also made a complex, disturbing, and fascinating statement about American ideals and ideologies. This book, accessible to all readers, provides us with the necessary tools to interpret and understand in historical perspective how the American advertising industry portrays anyone other than the white American mainstream—African Americans, Asians, women, Native Americans, tourists of many nationalities, all of whom have been treated as "the other"—in its print media.

With more than one hundred carefully selected illustrations, Professor O'Barr takes us on an enlightening excursion from two early American travel manuals (which so subtly and perhaps even unconsciously delineated a hegemonic ideology to the amateur American tourist-photographer), to advertisements in the 1929 *National Geographic* magazine, to Dennis O'Rourke's disturbing 1987 film *Cannibal Tours,* to images of blackness across the twentieth century, and on to the representation of the Japanese (and, conversely, their representation of white Americans) in contemporary times.

Though the author writes in a witty and readable style for the student and general reader, the argument he develops is one of profound seriousness: that the representation of foreigners and other categories of outsiders who appear in advertisements provides paradigms for relations between members of advertising's intended audience and those defined as outside of it. These paradigms constitute an ideological guide for relations—of hierarchy, dominance, and subordination—between self and others, between "us" and "them."

WILLIAM O'BARR is professor of cultural anthropology at Duke University. His publications include books on language in the American courtroom (*Linguistic Evidence,* 1982) and in the Third World (*Language and Politics,* 1976, with Jean F. O'Barr). He also has written about small claims courts (*Rules and Relationships,* 1990) and cultural change in Africa (*Tradition and Identity in Changing Africa,* 1972). Most recently he authored, with John M. Conley, an anthropological study of Wall Street titled *Fortune and Folly* (1992).

Index